Easy Guide to
Sewing Jackets

Cecelia Podolak

The Taunton Press

Cover Photo: Boyd Hagen
Back Cover Photos: Sloan Howard
Assisted by: Robert Marsala

Designer: Jodie Delohery
Layout Artist: Christopher Casey
Illustrator: Steve Buchanan
Typeface: Bookman/Optima
Paper: 70 lb. Warren Patina Matte
Printer: Quebecor Printing Hawkins, New Canton, Tennessee

Taunton
BOOKS & VIDEOS

for fellow enthusiasts

First printing: 1995
Second printing: 1996
Printed in the United States of America

A THREADS Book
THREADS® is a trademark of The Taunton Press, Inc.,
registered in the U.S. Patent and Trademark Office.

The Taunton Press, 63 South Main Street, Box 5506,
Newtown, CT 06470-5506

Library of Congress Cataloging-in-Publication Data

Podolak, Cecelia.
      Easy guide to sewing jackets / Cecelia Podolak.
          p. cm.
      "A Threads Book"
      Includes index.
      ISBN 1-56158-110-0
      1. Coats. I. Title.
TT535.P64 1995
646.4´3304—dc20   95-18165
                                              CIP

Introduction

Easy Guide to Sewing Jackets will teach you how to make classic collarless jackets. You will enhance your sewing skills, gain a better understanding of tailoring principles, and ultimately, create professional-looking jackets. Sewers of all levels will find this information useful, but it should be especially beneficial to those just beginning to make jackets or those coming back to sewing after being away for a while.

Jackets have long been one of my favorite garments, even though they haven't always been simple to make. My first jackets were custom-tailored blazers, shaped and molded to perfection with hand stitching. Fortunately, at the same time that my life became busier (and my sewing hours fewer), fast-and-easy industry techniques started gaining respectability among home sewers. We began exploiting the full capacities of our machines, working more rapidly, and finding ways to become proficient with ready-to-wear techniques. My students and I experimented with different marking techniques, fusible interfacings, and machine-sewing where possible. I soon realized that I could produce jackets in far less time, with results rivaling custom tailoring and better ready-to-wear. My sewing changed, and more and more people began asking where I had purchased my jackets.

Today, my jacket-making philosophy blends what I consider the best of traditional and contemporary techniques. I haven't discarded my hand-sewing needles, though I use them less frequently. Because I'm a slow sewer, I've streamlined jacket assembly methods where possible. A major leap in my efficiency came when I adopted the process method. This is a method for completing all similar tasks (such as cutting, marking, fusing, sewing, and pressing) at one time, rather than repeatedly working through these steps with each garment section. Initially this approach may be confusing, but it's really quite logical and will soon become second nature.

Easy Guide to Sewing Jackets is organized so you can work through the jacket-making process from the beginning stages of pattern and fabric selection, through decisions about interfacings and linings, to the best sewing and pressing techniques. Where possible, the focus is on industry methods. A professional-looking jacket is the primary objective, and I only suggest techniques that will give quality tailoring effects.

I encourage you to read through the entire book before beginning your project. Start slowly and follow the instructions to learn the proper techniques. Soon you'll be experimenting with more complicated styles and techniques—as well as acquiring a wardrobe that is uniquely yours.

1 Choosing Your Pattern

Which should you choose first—the fabric or the pattern? It's usually easiest to match a fabric to a pattern, so you must learn how to choose a pattern, from recognizing basic silhouettes to analyzing inner design details. Learn to identify which features complement your figure, your personal fashion sense, and your sewing skills. Once you've read this chapter and taken some measurements, you'll be ready to select the right pattern for your jacket project.

The biggest challenge when choosing a pattern is visualizing how the jacket will look on you. This can be difficult, so it's extremely useful for you to learn to "read" patterns. A photograph in a pattern book shows how a jacket looks once it's made up, but sometimes the silhouette is distorted, and often the essential inner details are hidden. It's easy to become sidetracked by a jacket's color or fabric and completely overlook the silhouette.

Study the drawings on the pattern envelope for a better idea of the jacket's silhouette, inner style lines, and garment details. Examine both the front and back views. Don't be afraid to open the pattern and inspect the guide sheet for the shapes of the pieces and any significant style details.

If you're unsure of what's best for you, or if you want to test your judgment, go shopping. Try on better-quality ready-to-wear jackets. Note the neckline lengths, sleeve styles, pocket style and placement, button placement, shaping darts and seams, and other details. Putting on the jackets and looking in a mirror is the best way to see what works and what doesn't. Then, while you still remember, go back to the pattern books and make your choice.

Think about what you will wear with your jacket, such as a matching or coordinating skirt, a dress, or pants. Be sure you'll have something that goes with it, because once your jacket is finished, you'll want to wear it right away.

Basic Jacket Silhouettes

For a jacket to be balanced throughout its width, the inner darts and seamlines always follow the outer silhouette: Patterns with straight side seams have no inner shaping, while curved side seams indicate curved inner darts or seams.

As you look through a pattern book, it's easy to become confused by so many styles, fabrics, colors, and details. Focus on the jacket's basic silhouette—not its details. You'll find that there are only a few basic jacket shapes or styles. Identify which ones are best for your figure type and which options meet your skill level, then narrow down your sleeve options. You'll find your jacket silhouette has taken shape.

Wearing and Design Ease

On the back of the pattern envelope you'll find either a description or a sketch of how the jacket is intended to fit—or how much ease the pattern contains. Understanding ease will help you decide which patterns best suit your personal style and figure type.

Wearing ease is necessary; it is the amount of fullness that was added to basic body measurements to allow you to move in the jacket. Because jackets may be worn alone or over other garments, styles vary in how much ease is added for comfort. Most pattern companies allow 2 in. to 3 in. of wearing ease in the bust and hip circumferences.

Design ease is the additional fullness that the designer added to give a jacket its particular style and flair. Pattern companies vary, but generally "designer" patterns have the most design ease. Loose-fitting, boxy jackets range from 5 in. to over 10 in. of design ease if the jacket is very loose; semi-fitted jackets typically have 3 in. to 4 in.; fitted jackets have little or no design ease (and a minimum amount of wearing ease as well).

CHOOSING JACKET STYLES

	Is this the best style for me?	Can I make it?
Boxy, with no darts ▼ ■ ▲	A boxy, unshaped jacket conceals many figure problems and is especially good for the fuller, rectangular body type. Extended or dropped shoulders help balance lower-body width. Position patch pockets low on the jacket to balance wide shoulders or a full bust.	This is the easiest jacket style to sew and fit, since it needs no real shaping. Its simplicity demands an interesting fabric texture, which can help conceal any uneven stitching. A boxy jacket makes a good choice for an unlined garment; there are few seams to finish, and the loose style makes it easy to put on and take off.
Semi-fitted with darts ✕ ■ ▲	A jacket slightly shaped with darts flatters many figures, but be careful of the length. Keep the jacket at or above hip level if you are petite, and lengthen it if you are tall.	Shaping a jacket with darts isn't difficult if you work carefully. Darts must fit the bust area, so mark and sew precisely. Consider a partial or full lining to allow the jacket to slip on and off easily.
Fitted with curved seams ✕ ▼	Princess lines highlight the body's curves. The waist shaping and outward curve of the lower edge helps balance broad shoulders or a full bust. Take care not to overfit this style.	A fitted jacket takes more time because there are more seams to fit and sew. The princess seam must fit the bust precisely, and curved seams must be clipped to lie flat. A full lining is best, because it conceals the seams.
Fitted with curved seams and darts ✕ ▼ ▲	Patch pockets above or below the waist help to balance this jacket on figures with slim hips or broad shoulders. Dart and seam fitting emphasize the waist. Be careful not to overfit.	Fit darts accurately at the bust and waist. Tapered stitching is needed to prevent bulges at dart tips. Use a full lining to cover seams and darts.

FIGURE TYPES

✕ Well-proportioned figure with definite waistline.

▲ Narrow shoulders, small bust compared to lower body.

▼ Broad shoulders, large bust with slim hip/thigh area.

■ Slender or full, with little waist definition. Fairly balanced shoulders and hips.

Sleeve Styles

Sleeves can be either separate pieces that are inserted into the garment body, such as set-in sleeves, or extensions of the jacket body itself, such as kimono or raglan sleeves. Regular set-in sleeves, the most common style, will always have smooth caps; dropped-shoulder, kimono, and raglan sleeves will always have folds or soft creases. Sleeve variations affect the jacket silhouette and can make your figure look either wider or narrower than it is.

Set-in Sleeves When looking at a sleeve pattern, visualize the capline, an imaginary line drawn across the sleeve from underarm to underarm that separates the sleeve cap from the rest of the sleeve. As the cap height lowers and widens, the sleeve begins to crease at the capline seam and underarm. If the set-in sleeve is divided with a vertical over-arm seam, the sleeve-cap ease may be incorporated into that seam and the cap may have no additional ease. This cap may crease diagonally. Below the capline, a one-

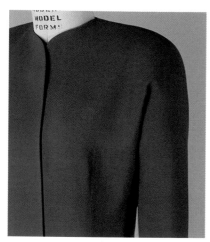

This kimono-sleeve jacket has a sleek silhouette because of the high-cut angle of the underarm.

SET-IN SLEEVES	High cap	Low cap
Distinguishing Features • Shoulder line	Slightly extended	Dropped 1 1/2 in. or more
• Sleeve cap shape	Maximum height, about 8 in., from capline to top of sleeve	Minimum height, 2 in. or less, from capline to top of sleeve
• Sleeve cap ease	Maximum ease: 1 1/2 in. to 2 in., smooth cap	Minimum or no ease, diagonal crease
• Underarm	High cut; smooth underarm and sleeve	Low cut, armhole and sleeve will crease
Effect on Body	Trim fit	Adds bulk and width
Skill Level	Requires precision easing and higher skill level	Good for beginners; sewn in flat
Best Fabric Type	Firmer, more sturdy	Softer, more drapable

piece sleeve may have a straight underarm seam with no shaping. This is the easiest sleeve to construct, but it widens the jacket silhouette. One-piece sleeves with the seam moved to the back are usually more shaped and are visually less widening. Two-piece sleeves with no underarm seam can be shaped for a trimmer, more tailored silhouette. The chart on the facing page compares high and low sleeve caps.

Interesting Details

Once you've decided on the basic silhouette and sleeve style that suits your skill level, begin to look at other design elements and how they will complement your body shape. For example, on a double-breasted style, the closer the two rows of buttons and the narrower the front overlap, the more slenderizing the jacket. A single button placed close to the waistline produces a longer line and creates an illusion of height. Jacket length should be in proportion to figure size and height: Shorter women should wear lengths ending above the hip; taller women will find below-the-hip lengths most flattering. Reexamine the pattern-envelope sketches and description. Some details, such as pockets, can be easily changed, while others, such as neckline angles, require more skill. The chart below describes details according to skill level.

Kimono and raglan sleeves differ primarily in the underarms. The raglan style retains the underarm of a set-in sleeve, resulting in a smoother underarm and silhouette. Kimono sleeves range from tailored and sleek to loose-fitting and fluid, depending upon the height and angle of the underarm curve and shoulder slope.

DETAILS AND SKILLS

If you are just beginning to sew jackets, try to use only the details from the first column. As you gain experience, add details from the second column. Don't let the jacket style overwhelm you; it's best to perfect a few details—and skills—at a time.

Easiest	More Challenging
Jewel or built-up neckline	Cardigan neckline
Kimono or dropped-shoulder, or two-piece sleeve with overarm seam	Set-in sleeve, one or two pieces with eased capline; raglan sleeve
Buttons along sleeve seam, no sleeve vent	Ready-to-wear sleeve vent
Unlined patch pocket or pocket flap only	Lined patch pocket, with or without flap
No buttons	Machine-made buttonholes
Curved front edges	Square front edges
No lining or partial lining	Full lining
No edgestitching or topstitching	Edgestitching and/or topstitching

Finding Your Size

Pattern sizing is well standardized, even though ease varies from one company to another. Also, pattern sizes and ready-to-wear sizes are completely different, so measure yourself carefully to find your correct size. Your pattern should fit well in the neck, upper chest, and armholes, since these areas are the trickiest to alter. Try to confine width alterations you make to the easy-to-change areas: the bust, waist, and hips.

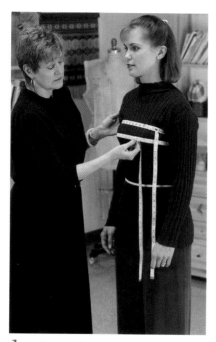

1 *Take two bust measurements: one around the fullest part and the other higher up, under the arms.*

If you are in between pattern sizes, consider your bone structure and the jacket style. Go down a size if your bone structure is fine and if jacket style is very loose fitting. But if the jacket is fitted, it's probably best to go up a size, simply because fitted jackets have little or no ease.

How to Measure

To select your pattern size, compare your high-bust and full-bust measurements. If your full bust is 2 in. or more larger than your high bust, purchase by your high-bust measurement. This will give you a pattern that fits in the hard-to-alter areas, and you may only need to let out underarm seams for the bust. The waist, hip, and back-waist measurements are listed on the pattern envelope for comparison. Check the front-waist and sleeve measurements when you pin-fit your pattern. Take your measurements over well-fitting undergarments. Tie a piece of ¼-in. elastic around your waist to define it better before you measure.

Full bust and high bust: Measure around the fullest part of the bust, across the back; pull snug. Measure high under the arms, across the chest and the widest part of the back; pull snug **(1)**.

Waist: Measure at the narrowest curve to find your natural waist.

Front waist: Measure from the top of your shoulder over the bust point to your waistline **(2)**. Also note the distance from shoulder to bust point.

Back waist: Measure vertically from the most prominent bone at the base of your neck to your waist **(3)**.

Hips: With tape measure parallel to the floor, measure around the fullest part of the hips. Note the distance from waist to hip **(4)**.

Sleeve: Bend your arm and measure from the shoulder bone, around your elbow, to just below your wrist **(5)**.

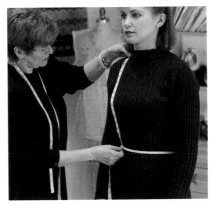

2 *Measure from the top of your shoulder to your waistline.*

3 *Measure from the base of your neck to your waist.*

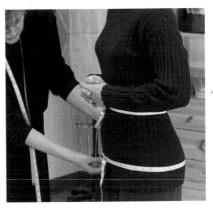

4 *Measure around the fullest part of the hips.*

5 *Bend your arm and measure from your shoulder bone to your wrist.*

MULTISIZE PATTERNS

Multisize patterns come with three or more sizes printed and graded on one tissue. Use a felt-tip marker to trace the outline you will follow when cutting. Be careful at neck and armhole curves, where the lines shift position: Lines for the larger sizes that were at the outermost position move to the inside at these places. These patterns are terrific for those without perfectly proportioned figures because width alterations that would require cutting inside the pattern can sometimes be entirely eliminated. For example, to fit a figure that is wider at the bottom, first outline the pattern in the neck/shoulder/armhole area, then increase to a larger size at the underarm to accommodate a fuller bust, and finally increase to a still larger size at the hips. Always merge cutting lines gradually, and avoid abrupt changes from one size to another.

Some patterns have a ⅝-in. seam allowance on each piece, but usually it isn't marked. Mark the allowances for pin-fitting using a ⅝-in. wide tape measure. For other patterns with no seam allowances, either add tissue paper for 1-in. allowances, or butt the seamlines together and tape with removable tape.

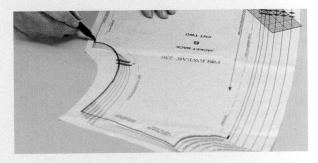

2 Selecting Fabrics and Notions

Once you've chosen your pattern, the next step is to find fabric, lining, interfacing, and notions that will work with it. Here is a guide for selecting and preparing these items for sewing and identifying the notions that will make your work more efficient.

Fabrics that are difficult to sew or press can frustrate the most experienced sewer, even if the pattern is simple. Learn to recognize which fabrics will guarantee a successful jacket and which ones may cause problems, perhaps because of their drape, weight, weave, or texture. Use fiber content, surface texture, and fabric resilience as guides for choosing fabrics for your first project.

Whether you line your jacket completely, partially, or not at all depends on your pattern and fashion fabric and how much time you want to spend. Unlined or partially lined jackets are great when you're in a hurry and you want a casual style; keep in mind, however, that you'll have to finish the exposed seam allowances. If you enjoy a truly fine finish, line your jacket completely.

In the last 20 years, interfacings have changed dramatically. Today's tailoring relies on fusible rather than sew-in interfacings. Fusibles have improved enormously, so if you are hesitant to use them because of previous problems, consider giving them another try. If you use the guidelines in this chapter to identify fusibles that are suitable for jacket-weight fabrics and you always make test samples, your interfacing should be trouble-free.

Some seemingly small features have a large visual and structural impact on your jacket. Certain finishing details, such as proper shoulder pads, give your jacket a polished, professionally finished appearance. Consider these items carefully, and also the notions you will need for cutting, marking, and sewing. The right tools make the job easier—and far more fun!

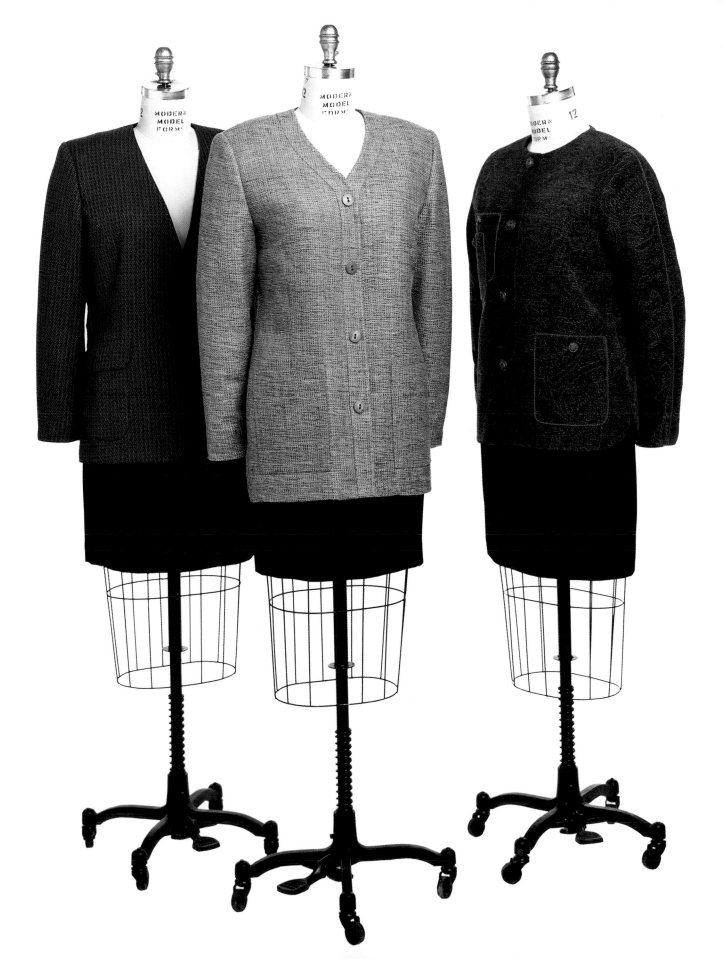

Choosing Fabrics

Fabrics should be easy to work with, complementing the jacket's design and pattern complexity. Look for a medium-weight fabric with a firm weave that resists wrinkling, surface snagging, and shifting yarns. Linings conceal inner construction details while providing support and durability, and they can add a splash of color or pattern whenever they are exposed.

Fashion Fabric Options

Softness, firmness, fineness, and resilience all combine to produce a fabric's hand, or drape. Structured cardigan-style jackets with regular set-in sleeves will usually demand firmer fabrics than kimono-style jackets, for example. When exploring your fabric options, stand before a mirror and drape the fabric over your shoulder. How does it fall on your body? How does it look from a distance?

Wool is traditionally the first-choice fabric for jackets.

Wool: Wool, because it can be shaped and molded, is the traditional tailoring choice for easy jackets. The first choice is 100% wool; barring that, find a blend of at least 50% wool. *Woolens* are made from low-twist yarns, have a soft drape, are easy to press, and hide sewing imperfections. *Worsteds*, such as gabardine and serge, are woven with tightly twisted yarns that result in a durable finish and a crisp, resilient hand. Unfortunately, they are difficult to press, and sewing mistakes show clearly.

Expanding your options: Other fibers and fiber blends may also make good choices. Cotton, silk, rayon, and linen sew and press beautifully, but the finished jacket may wrinkle easily. If wrinkles bother you, consider a fabric that blends these fibers with polyester, nylon, or wool for wrinkle resistance. Or consider 100% polyester and microfiber (polyester, rayon, or nylon) fabrics, but realize that these demand topstitching and edgestitching because pressing sharp seams and edges is difficult.

First-project choices: Fabrics with a surface texture, such as tweeds or bouclés are good choices because they conceal sewing imperfections. Consider small multicolor woven checks, prints, or jacquards that don't need exact matching or precise placement. Avoid smooth, solid-color fabrics, at least for a first project, since they show every sewing and pressing detail.

On-grain ends: If possible, have your fabric torn from the bolt when you buy it to ensure that the ends are on grain. When fabric is cut, the ends must be straightened by following a yarn across the fabric width and either pulling it or cutting along it. When the fabric is folded, both layers of the fabric should form a right angle at each end. This may not always happen, and it may be necessary to pull on the diagonal, from one short corner to the other. If this does not completely align the layers, steam-press the fabric on the diagonal.

Preshrinking: It's a good idea to preshrink all fabrics. Most dry cleaners will steam-shrink fabrics for a nominal per-yard fee, or you can preshrink natural-fiber fabrics, such as wool, silk, linen, and cottons, at home with an iron that produces a lot of steam: Press with a raising-and-lowering motion on the wrong side, letting the fabric dry before moving to another section, and supporting the fabric ends to prevent stretching.

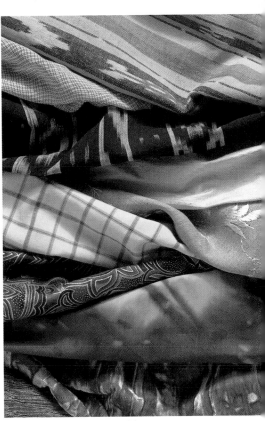

Cotton, silk, rayon, and linen sew beautifully but tend to wrinkle.

Polyester and other synthetics are heat-set and may resist alignment. Follow the lengthwise grain for pattern placement and consider cutting each piece on a single layer of fabric.

Consider both regular and nonstandard lining fabrics. If you choose a lighter lining fabric, be sure it is opaque enough to cover the inside details.

Lining Choices

Lining fabrics are available in a variety of fibers. My favorites are luxurious bemberg rayon and lightweight acetate-rayon blends, because they allow the body to breathe. When you press, use a lower iron temperature and very little steam. Medium-weight acetate twills, jacquards, and plain-weave fabrics are also comfortable to wear and cover inner details nicely. Heavyweight satin linings are better for outdoor jackets and coats. Polyester linings are durable, inexpensive, and washable. Read the bolt end to find the breathable antistatic polyesters.

LINING OPTIONS				
Sleeve style	Unlined	Sleeves lined	Partially lined	Fully lined
Set-In		X	X	X
Dropped shoulder	X	X	X	X
Kimono	X			X
Raglan	X		X	X

Don't rule out blouse and dress fabrics, especially if you want a printed or patterned lining. Again, breathable polyesters are best. Rayon wrinkles unless it's blended with polyester, and some rayons may not be slippery enough. For the ultimate in luxury, treat yourself to silk charmeuse, satin-backed silk crepe, or even a sueded silk. Though more expensive and less durable than regular lining fabrics, these should last for the life of the jacket.

Preshrink lining fabric with a steam iron (see page 17), being careful not to drip water on the fabric, since it may spot (especially bemberg and some silks). Hand-washing rayon may cause a crinkled effect that won't iron out, and it isn't necessary if the jacket will be dry cleaned. I prefer to dry clean my lined jackets (including those made of washable fabrics), since it's difficult to press a jacket after washing it.

Lining Styles Your choices don't end with the fabric; you also get to elect where your jacket will be lined. Full linings cover the entire interior; partial linings cover the upper back and chest and/or the sleeves. Unlined jackets give an unstructured, casual look.

Your jacket's sleeve style influences not only the type of fashion fabric to be used, but also how a jacket will be lined. For example, unlined jackets require roomy sleeves and smooth fabrics so they are easy to slide on and off. Use the chart on the facing page to help you decide how your jacket should be lined. If you want to revise your lining pattern or assemble a new one, see pages 36–38.

Jackets with set-in sleeves and high-cut underarms are most comfortable if the sleeves are lined. Lined sleeves are not as critical in dropped-shoulder styles, because their lower underarm roominess provides greater ease of movement. Kimono styles have no armhole seam for attaching a partial lining, and so should be either fully lined or left unlined. Raglan sleeves are cut as one piece with the upper jacket front and back but have the curved underarm shaping of a set-in sleeve. Consider a full or partial lining, rather than trying to line only the sleeves.

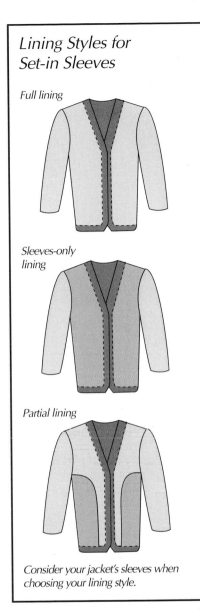

Lining Styles for Set-in Sleeves

Full lining

Sleeves-only lining

Partial lining

Consider your jacket's sleeves when choosing your lining style.

Interfacings and Notions

Thanks to the garment industry and its quest for more efficient production, we have fusible interfacings—fabrics coated with resin that are pressed and fused onto the jacket fabric. Shoulder pads support the jacket and let it hang the way the designer intended. There are also some notions you won't want to do without, for making your jacket and to have on hand as basic sewing equipment.

Interfacings

Ideally, interfacing supports and shapes the jacket without substantially changing the fabric's original drape. It stabilizes front edges, pockets, and hems; shapes sleeve caps; and reinforces buttons and buttonholes. Similar interfacings carry different brand names, so it's much easier to identify them by their fabric construction. There are four types of interfacings: woven, nonwoven, and tricot knit—all of which may be fusible or sew-in—and weft-insertion, a knitted fabric stabilized with an additional yarn, which is always fusible.

Finding the Right One For a softly tailored jacket, try fusible tricot knits and lightweight weft-insertions. These remain flexible when fused and keep the fashion fabric from becoming too rigid. Jacket-weight weft-insertions and some nonwovens will remain flexible but usually give the fabric a firmer drape. Using woven and most nonwoven fusibles results in a relatively rigid fabric. For heat-sensitive microfibers and other synthetics, consider the low-melt fusibles.

Recommending any particular fusible is difficult. Resin reacts differently with all fabrics, dyes, and finishes, and each jacket style has different needs. The only foolproof way to find the best interfacing for your project is to test-fuse it to the fashion fabric.

Interfacings by fabric construction, top to bottom: Weft-insertion, woven, nonwoven, hair canvas, and tricot knit.

Testing Different Fusibles First preshrink the interfacing: Soak woven, knit, and weft-insertion interfacings in hot tap water for 20 minutes. Fold carefully, blot with a towel, then dry over the shower rod. To test-fuse, cut an 8-in. square of fashion fabric and two 3-in.-squares of fusible interfacing. Pink one side of the interfacing squares before fusing to compare with the unpinked side. Pinking softens the interfacing line and helps prevent ridges on the fashion fabric's right side. Fuse test samples on one half of the 8-in. square. Fold the unbonded half over the interfacing as a facing, then fold the two interfacings together to judge their combined thickness.

With the test sample, you can compare the drape, surface texture, and color of the interfaced fashion fabric to the original, as well as how well the interfacing adheres to the fabric surface. The fashion fabric should retain as much of its original character as possible, and the interfacing should not bubble or bleed through to the right side. The sides with the pinked edges should lie smooth. If you're still unsure after test-fusing several different interfacings, it's safest to go with the one that gives the softest feel. If you find a fusible absolutely won't work, you'll need to resort to a sew-in.

FINDING THE RIGHT SHOULDER PAD

Select the shoulder pad that enhances your pattern's sleeve style: For a standard set-in sleeve with a slightly extended shoulder, choose a straight-outer-edge pad (see left pad in photo); for dropped-shoulder, kimono, or raglan sleeves, find a curved pad that molds over the shoulder (see right pad in photo).

These shoulder-pad shapes also come in various thicknesses. Adhere to your pattern's suggested thickness, since the jacket and sleeve were designed to accommodate a pad of this height.

An unlined pad of cotton or polyester batting molds to the body better than foam rubber. Unlined pads may be covered for unlined jackets.

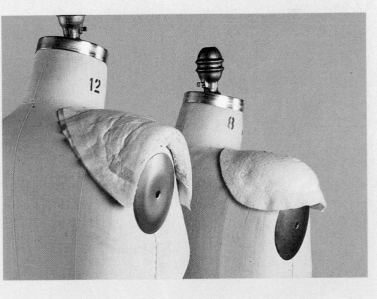

Invaluable Notions for Sewing

There are many notions available to make sewing projects easier. Be sure you purchase them before you begin your jacket project, so everything you need for a smooth execution is at hand.

Basting tape: Narrow, double-sided transparent tape that holds two pieces of fabric together for stitching; if water soluble, you can machine-stitch through it.

Beeswax: Wax for strengthening thread in hand-sewing, especially for sewing on buttons.

Buttonhole cutter: A sharp metal tool for cutting through several layers of fabric to open a buttonhole.

Dressmakers' tracing paper and wheel: Paper and tool for transferring pattern markings to wrong side of fabric. Some

papers are wax-free or air-soluble (marks disappear in a short time).

Machine needles: Use size 80/90 universal for most jacket fabrics and microtex sharps for microfibers. If you use buttonhole twist or doubled thread, use a size 100 topstitching needle.

Pattern weights: Special weights for holding the pattern pieces to the fabric, in lieu of pins (except for holding grainline in place).

Pinking shears: Scissors with a zigzag edge for finishing seams and edges, notching fabric from curved corners, and "softening" interfacing inner edges.

Pins: Extra long (1⅜-in.) pins are superior for thick fabrics.

Pocket template: A metal guide with four curved corners for shaping patch pockets with curved corners.

Point turner: Plastic or bamboo tool for pushing out corners. Some also have a notched area for lifting buttons to make shanks.

Rotary cutter and mat: A round-bladed tool for cutting fabric that works like a pizza cutter, used with a special mat. Cut freehand around curves, or with a ruler on straight edges. Some rotary cutters have pinking or scalloped edges.

Sewing gauge: A 6-in. ruler with a sliding marker; keep by the machine for quickly checking seam widths, and so on.

Space Tape marking tape: Special tape used for accurate buttonhole placement and size. Stabilizes buttonholes as they are being stitched.

Straight Tape topstitching tape: 1-in. wide tape marked for sewing perfectly straight topstitching.

Tailor's chalk, marking pencils, and pens: Tools for transferring pattern markings or making adjustments directly onto fabric.

Thread: Cotton-covered polyester and 100% polyester threads work well with most fabrics; select the one that matches your fabric (but a bit darker to blend in better). Microfiber fabrics may require a fine cotton thread.

Transparent ruler: A 2-in. by 18-in. clear ruler that is useful in altering and revising patterns.

3 | *Fitting Your Pattern*

Your project is organized. Now it's time to get down to the nitty-gritty: pattern work. This can be quite exciting, because you get to be the designer and revise the pieces to make them more workable. *Adjustments*, such as lengthening or shortening the waist, make the pattern fit better; *refinements*, such as redesigning the pockets, change the pattern's structure or style. Now you will learn when and how to make both kinds of revisions.

Traditionally, a test jacket was made of muslin, to custom-fit the pattern before cutting the jacket pattern pieces from expensive fabric. Unless your measurements are quite disproportionate, however, it's not necessary to make a muslin test copy of your jacket. I prefer a technique called "pin-fitting"—pinning the tissue pattern together and then placing it on the body. You'll learn more about your pattern and body with this method and have the opportunity to make many different changes. For most women, pin-fitting is all that is needed to obtain a good fit from a standard jacket pattern.

If pattern adjustments seem difficult to you and possibly even intimidating, you are not alone. But if you take them one step at a time, you'll find most of them are rather simple. First I will address basic length and width adjustments that can be made before pin-fitting. Other fitting problems will show up when the pattern is on the body. Then, once your jacket pattern is altered, you can refine interfacing and lining pieces according to the amount of structure you want in the jacket. Here you will see how easy it is to make lining pieces if none came with your pattern, or how to revise an existing lining pattern so you can insert the entire lining with the sewing machine.

Precision is the key to successful fitting, so strive for accuracy rather than speed. Your reward will be a jacket that fits you as no ready-made ever could, and you'll gain a set of fitting skills that can be used repeatedly.

Adjusting the Pattern

Compare your body measurements to those on the pattern and make basic length and width changes. Length changes to the jacket body and sleeve are the easiest. After these, address width. A few small changes will allow the pattern to fit your body better and will aid in pin-fitting.

Adjustment Guidelines

Here are some guidelines for successful pattern alteration:

• Before checking any measurements, cut out the pattern pieces and press all creases flat with a warm, dry iron.

• Be sure stitching lines are marked on the tissue so they can be used as reference points for adjustments and pin-fitting.

• Keep a record of what you alter, and by how much.

• Keep in mind that once the tissue is altered, the pattern must remain flat for cutting.

• Keep straight-of-grain arrows straight and parallel to the center front or center back, and perpendicular to the hemline.

• Most patterns have lengthening/shortening line; be sure the grainline arrow extends through them before cutting them apart.

- Make the same alterations on all adjoining pattern sections.

- Make only one adjustment at a time, to avoid confusion.

- Always test the altered pattern by pinning it together and fitting it on your body before cutting any fabric.

Lengthening

On a strip of tissue paper as wide as the pattern piece and at least 1 in. longer than the necessary alteration amount, draw two parallel horizontal lines, with space between them equal to the additional length.

Cut the pattern apart at the main lengthening/shortening line. Match and tape the upper portion to the top line on the tissue. Extend the grainline onto the tissue. Tape the lower pattern section below the bottom line on the tissue, matching grainline markings. Redraw any seamlines affected by the adjustment.

Shortening

Draw a new parallel line above the lengthening/shortening line printed on the pattern, at a distance that equals the amount to be shortened. Fold the lower line and bring it to the upper one, keeping grainlines aligned. Tape in place. Redraw any seamlines affected by the alteration.

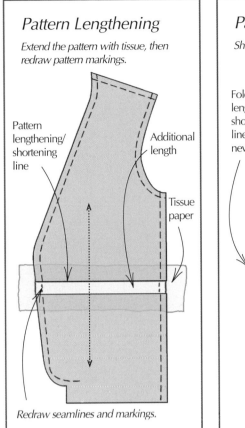

Pattern Lengthening

Extend the pattern with tissue, then redraw pattern markings.

Pattern lengthening/ shortening line

Additional length

Tissue paper

Redraw seamlines and markings.

Pattern Shortening

Shorten your pattern with simple folds.

Fold pattern lengthening/ shortening line up to new line

Redraw seamlines and markings.

Adding Width

Measure the pattern pieces between the seam allowances to obtain the total width of the bust, waist, and hips. If you need only 2 in. to 2½ in. of additional width in these areas, divide this amount by the number of vertical seams in the jacket.

Increase the width of the pattern up to ⅝ in. at the outside seams in the respective areas, tapering new seamlines back to the original seamlines when necessary. Add this same extra width to the lining pieces. If you need to add more than 2½ in. for a fuller bust, alter between the seamlines of the pattern (as on page 31) so that other proportions are retained.

RETAINING DESIGN EASE

Before starting any width alterations, check the total circumference of the bust, just below the underarm area, and hips, 7 in. to 9 in. below the waist. Some pattern companies print this on the bust and hip pattern pieces. If your pattern doesn't have this information, measure the front and back from side seam to center front and center back, respectively, taking care not to measure over dart. Double this measure to obtain the total jacket circumference. Since the minimum amount of wearing ease in the bust and hips is 2 in. to 3 in., subtract this from the total circumference for each area. The result tells you how much design ease your jacket contains.

If you use part of the design ease to increase bust and hip width, rather than adding additional width as described, you may destroy the jacket's style. If your pattern is extremely loose fitting, you may be able to use some of the design ease, but it's still a risk. Check your pattern fit carefully before going down a size.

Measure to find how much design ease is in your pattern.

Increasing the Hem Depth

A 2-in. deep bottom hem provides weight and quality to the finished jacket and also makes easy work of bagging the lining. For a lined jacket, the hem should be 2 in.; for an unlined jacket, at least 1½ in. Sleeve hems vary from 1½ in. to 2 in. deep. Check and revise your pattern for adequate hems.

Widening Seam Allowances

Wide seam allowances are easier to press, and they lie flatter in the garment. They also provide a bit of security: If you make any errors in pin-fitting, you'll have more room for corrections. You can widen seam allowances as you cut the fabric if you won't need the additional tissue for pin-fitting. Increase the shoulder, side, center back, and sleeve underarm seam allowances from ⅝ in. to 1 in. Do not widen allowances of sharply curved seams (such as armholes or necklines) or front edges.

Pin-Fitting the Pattern

Pinning the jacket pattern pieces together and fitting them on the body replaces the time-consuming method of cutting and sewing the jacket in muslin. Although pattern tissue does not fit like fabric, it drapes the body well enough to give you a good idea of the jacket's fit. Pin-fitting is hard to do alone, so try to recruit a friend to help.

Assembling the Tissue Pattern

Press narrow strips of fusible interfacing to armhole and neckline curves to prevent pattern from tearing. Then pin the pattern pieces with wrong sides together, inserting the pins on and parallel to the seamlines. This leaves seam and dart allowances showing on the pattern's right side, making adjustments easier to see and mark.

Clip all curves to the stitching line (neckline, armhole, side waist) so that the pattern will lie flat on the body. Pin up jacket and sleeve hems, folding the hem allowance to the right side of the pattern.

Pin the shoulder seams, vertical seams, and all darts on the jacket body, following stitching lines as accurately as possible. The back shoulder is usually eased to the front. Do not pin beyond the seam-allowance intersections where shoulder and vertical seams cross (neckline and underarm).

Pin the sleeve underarm seam so it is ready to attach once the jacket body is pin-fitted.

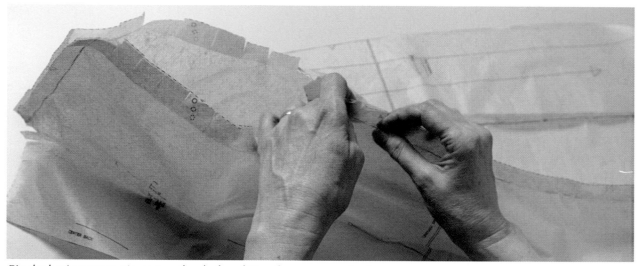

Pin the basic pattern pieces together before fitting them on your body.

If you fit your pattern alone, first pin the pattern tissue to a shoulder pad, then pin it on yourself. You can anchor the center back using double-sided tape, and anchor the center front with pins.

Fitting the Tissue Pattern

To make your fitting as accurate as possible, wear clothing that you might actually wear under your finished jacket. Pin or tape the jacket's shoulder pads to your shoulders, extending them slightly over the shoulder to simulate the jacket style.

Carefully slip on the prepared tissue. Anchor the pattern to your clothing with pins at center front and center back, aligning them with the centers of your body and your waistline. Check the fit, working from the top down and from front to back, following the steps shown below and on the following pages.

When your fitting is complete, unpin and flatten the pattern to alter it where you have marked. Be sure to alter the jacket, facings, and lining pieces in similar ways.

Shoulder: The shoulder seam should rest on top of, and extend $\frac{1}{4}$ in. to $\frac{1}{2}$ in. beyond, the shoulder (**1**). To lengthen or shorten, slash diagonally from the shoulder seam to the armhole notch, beginning about 2 in. from the armhole seam. Spread or lap the necessary amount and redraw seam.

Front chest: The neck opening may gape if the distance from the shoulder to the bust area is too

1 *Is the shoulder seam wide enough and properly positioned?*

long. To correct, fold a horizontal tuck between the bust and shoulder, tapering to nothing at the armhole seam **(2)**. True the front chest from the neck to the top button, then make the same corrections on the facing.

Bust: If the bodice width is too snug, diagonal wrinkles will form around the bust and pattern will pull away from center front. If you have widened side seam allowances to 1 in., you can now safely let them out ½ in. to ⅝ in., tapering to the original seamline at the waist or hem. Also adjust the sleeve underarm seam to correspond to the jacket width, tapering to the wrist. If more than ⅝ in. is needed, alter according to the sketch.

Darts: Horizontal darts should angle upward and end approximately 1 in. from the bust point (where the bust is most prominent) **(3)**. Vertical darts may align with the bust point or slightly to the side, and may end ½ in. from the bust point. Princess styles have curved seams but no dart fitting, and the bust falls in the

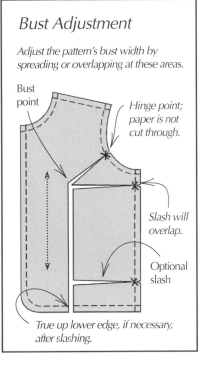

Bust Adjustment

Adjust the pattern's bust width by spreading or overlapping at these areas.

Bust point

Hinge point; paper is not cut through.

Slash will overlap.

Optional slash

True up lower edge, if necessary, after slashing.

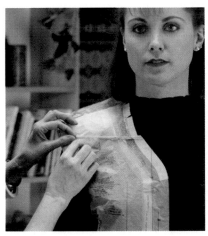

2 *A horizontal tuck will smooth a gaping neckline.*

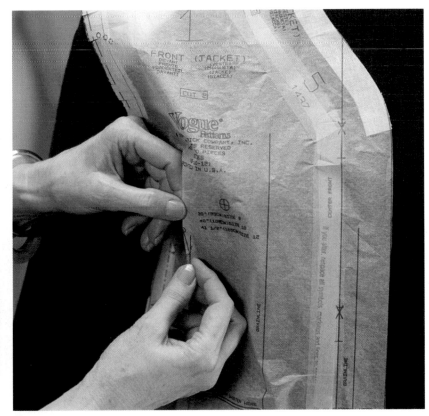

3 *Check dart placement throughout the bodice.*

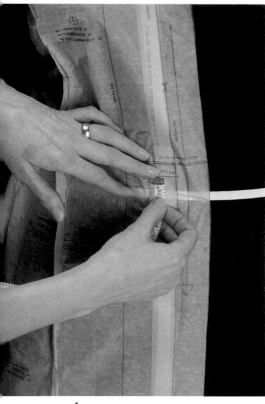

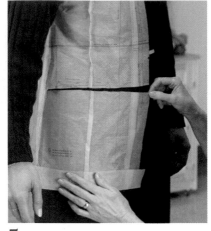

5 *A slash just below the waist adds extra room for a large tummy.*

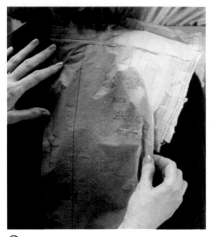

6 *Take a tuck near the armhole to ensure proper fit. Take a small horizontal tuck to eliminate excess length in the jacket back, then check for ease.*

4 *The pattern waist should fall at your natural waist.*

outward curve of the princess seam. Lengthen or shorten for this curve between the armhole and the full part of the bust.

Waist: Do the waistline markings coincide with your body's waistline? If not, lengthen or shorten the pattern between the bust and waist on the jacket front, back, and facing **(4)**.

Abdomen: A tummy bulge causes the side seams to swing forward and the front hem to swing upward. To adjust, cut and spread the pattern 2 in. to 3 in. below the waist, tapering to nothing at the side seam **(5)**. Then true the center-front line: Carry the original line (above the waist) straight down to the hem.

Hip and side seams: Side seams should hang perfectly straight from the underarm. If this area is too tight, let side seams out at the front and back hip, tapering up to the original underarm seamline (unless you changed this width earlier, in

bust adjustments). If the side seam swings toward the back, let out the back seam only.

Upper back and shoulders: Excess length is to blame if a horizontal wrinkle forms just below the neck. To remove it, fold a small horizontal tuck at center back, tapering to nothing at the armhole. Then realign the center back seam, from the neck to the waist. Is there adequate ease across the shoulder blade area? If you can pinch a $1/2$-in. tuck close to the armhole **(6)**, the ease should be fine. If not, this alteration is similar to the bust alteration except the vertical slash extends to the shoulder seam about 2 in. from the armhole. The upper horizontal slash goes across to the armhole where the extra width is needed—usually at the armhole notches.

Center back: With a swayback, the center-back seam below the waist shifts toward the side, and the side seams swing forward. At the waist, fold a horizontal tuck at center

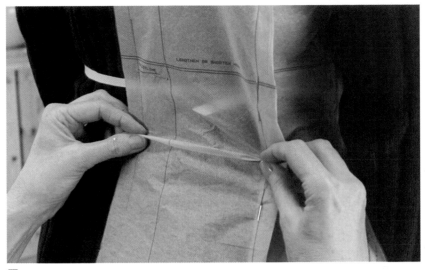

7 *Take a tuck below the waistline to adjust pattern for swayback.*

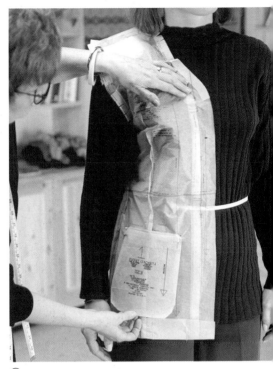

8 *Position the pockets and check jacket length.*

back, tapering to nothing at the side seam **(7)**. Then true the center back line: Carry the original line (above the waist) straight down to the hem. Add half of the tucked amount back to the center back lower edge, tapering to nothing at the side seam.

Final details: Adjust the pockets (placement and size) and the jacket length, as the style and your comfort prescribe **(8)**. Check that front button placement coincides with stress points at either the bust or waist.

Sleeve: Check the fit in the jacket underarm area, then slip the sleeve over your arm. Match and pin the sleeve cap to the jacket at the front and back armhole notches only. If you can pinch a 1½-in. vertical tuck in the sleeve, there is sufficient wearing ease. Check this in both the upper and lower parts of the sleeve. Pull the top of the sleeve cap up to the shoulder seam to check sleeve length **(9)**. Personal preference should dictate: I like the hem about ½ in. below my wrist bone.

9 *Pin sleeve onto jacket body and check upper and lower parts of sleeve for fit. Fold cuff to assess hem width and sleeve length.*

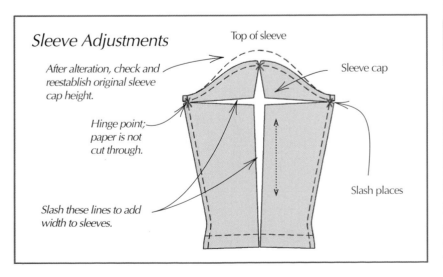

Sleeve Adjustments

Top of sleeve

Sleeve cap

After alteration, check and reestablish original sleeve cap height.

Hinge point; paper is not cut through.

Slash these lines to add width to sleeves.

Slash places

Refining the Pattern

The outer structure of the jacket is determined by the shape and placement of the interfacing and lining. Even though your pattern guide will suggest specifics, learn to rely on your own judgment for revising pattern pieces. Use this section to personalize your jacket and make it what you want it to be.

Shoulder pad width is a consideration when modifying or making a lining.

Interfacing Decisions

For the most structure, fuse firmer interfacing on the jacket body, and lighter, more flexible interfacing on the facings. For a softer look in casual, unstructured, unlined or partially lined jackets, fuse interfacing only to the facings. Lightweight interfacings are almost always used for hems, upper back, and shoulder overlays. Mix and match interfacings to get the look you want.

Your pattern may or may not include separate pieces for cutting interfacings, but don't despair—you can use your pattern pieces. For layout, the interfacing grainline generally matches that of the fashion fabric. Cut interfacing pieces with seam and dart allowances, and then study your test sample to decide whether or not to trim them off. Ready-to-wear manufacturers leave allowances in; it's faster and keeps fabrics from raveling.

Interfacings for Lined or Partially Lined Jackets

Cut and place interfacing for a lined jacket as shown. Soften edges of interfacing by pinking.

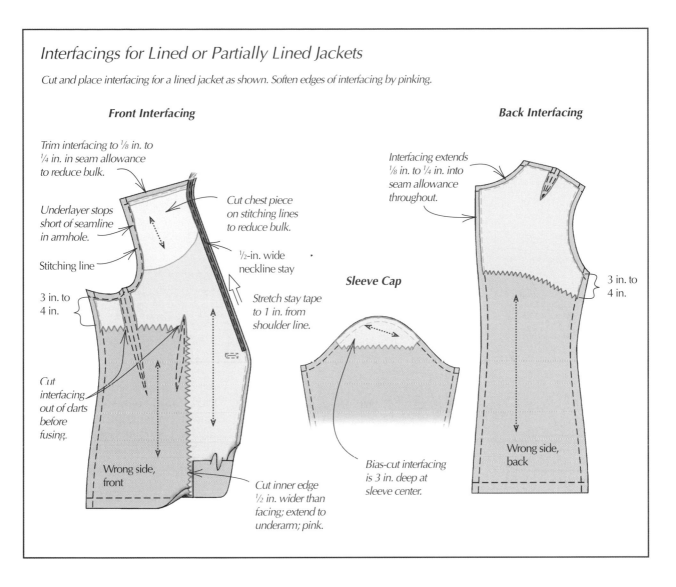

Front Interfacing

Trim interfacing to 1/8 in. to 1/4 in. in seam allowance to reduce bulk.

Underlayer stops short of seamline in armhole.

Stitching line

3 in. to 4 in.

Cut interfacing out of darts before fusing.

Wrong side, front

Cut chest piece on stitching lines to reduce bulk.

1/2-in. wide neckline stay

Stretch stay tape to 1 in. from shoulder line.

Cut inner edge 1/2 in. wider than facing; extend to underarm; pink.

Sleeve Cap

Bias-cut interfacing is 3 in. deep at sleeve center.

Back Interfacing

Interfacing extends 1/8 in. to 1/4 in. into seam allowance throughout.

3 in. to 4 in.

Wrong side, back

Interfacing for a Lined Jacket Cut the front interfacing, following the shape of the front facing, curving outward toward the underarm, ending 3 in. to 4 in. below the cut edge. For a lined jacket, cut the inner straight edge 1/2 in. wider than the facing to buffer the facing edge.
Layering an extra chest piece over the front interfacing fills the shoulder hollow. Follow the seamlines of the shoulder line and down two-thirds of the armhole length. Gently curve toward the front edge, then follow along the front neck. Fuse this layered piece as you did for the bottom piece.

For the back interfacing, follow the neck, shoulder, and armhole, then stop at center back, 8 in. to 10 in. below the neck edge. Curve gently downward to the side seam, ending 3 in. to 4 in. below the cut edge.

Cut front and back neck facings according to pattern pieces.

Small pieces of interfacing can be layered on top of larger pieces to give more support to specific sections, such as the chest and shoulders. To avoid excess rigidity, layer with a lighter weight interfacing, trim the seam allowances completely away, and cut the pieces on the bias grain.

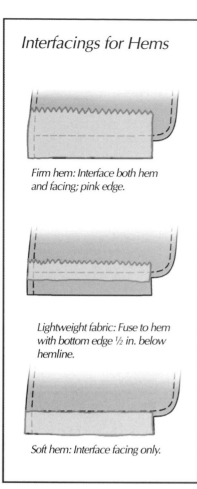
You have three options for interfacing the jacket and sleeve hems:

1. For a firm hem, cut strips twice the hem width plus ½ in. Place the strips so that a hem depth plus ½ in. extends above the hem fold line. This extra width extends upward into the jacket body, buffering the hem's cut edge.

2. To support lightweight or soft fabric without making the hem too firm, cut strips the hem width plus 1 in. Place the strip on the jacket body, extending ½ in. into the hem facing.

3. For a soft hem, cut strips the hem width and apply them to the hem facing.

If you want to add an easy ready-to-wear sleeve vent, see the diagrams on pages 79-81. Interface the sleeve vent from the outer cut edge to fold and placement lines on the sleeve pattern.

For patch pockets, use the same interfacing as for the jacket fronts. Cut pockets on the lengthwise grain for best support.

For greater flexibility in some places (such as the hem and upper back), use the bias grain, except for tricot knit, which stretches most in the crosswise grain. Garment manufacturers have recently used lightweight woven stitch-in interfacing, cut on the bias, in these places. Batiste, organza, or muslin can also be used.

Interfacing for an Unlined Jacket Cut the fronts and back using the facing pattern pieces. Follow instructions for a soft hem, as described above.

Making and Modifying the Lining

You can leave your jacket unlined, line it completely, or line it only partially. Review the chart on page 18 if you still need to make this decision. A lining pattern may not come with your pattern, but the steps below explain how to design one. If your pattern does include a lining, make sure it is suited for the bagging technique: Overlay the lining pieces on the jacket pieces, and check it as if you were making a new lining. A back-neck facing is essential for the bagging technique, and you will need to design one if there is none in the pattern. If the pattern requires shoulder pads, don't forget to take this into account when you adapt the jacket pattern to create the lining pattern. To line only your jacket's sleeves, follow the instructions on the facing page for cutting a lining sleeve. The inside of your unlined jacket will look more finished if you cover the shoulder pads, as described on page 39.

Making a Pattern for a Full Lining Cut all lining pieces ½ in. to ⅝ in. beyond the finished jacket length to produce a small ease tuck when the lining is sewn. If you are unsure about the jacket's fit, leave 1 in. side and shoulder seam allowances. As for interfacing, use the same grainline

Cutting Lining from Jacket Pattern Pieces

If your pattern does not come with lining pieces, make them yourself.

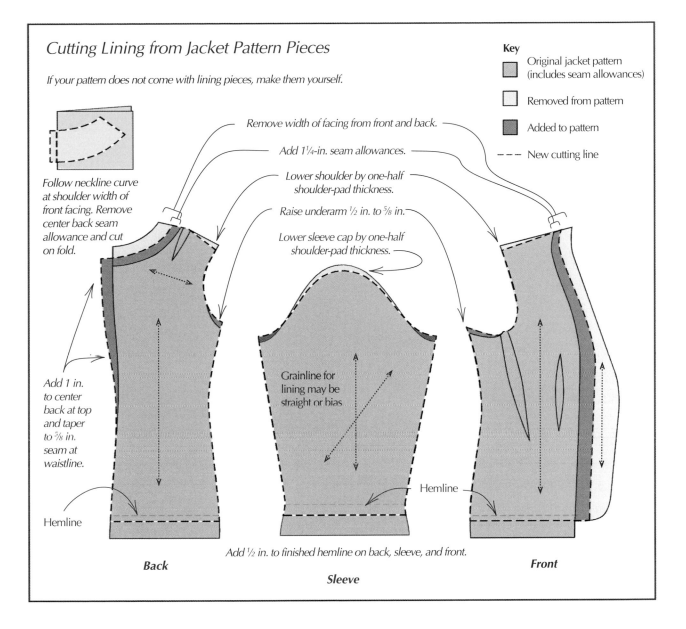

Follow neckline curve at shoulder width of front facing. Remove center back seam allowance and cut on fold.

Remove width of facing from front and back.

Add 1¼-in. seam allowances.

Lower shoulder by one-half shoulder-pad thickness.

Raise underarm ½ in. to ⅝ in.

Lower sleeve cap by one-half shoulder-pad thickness.

Add 1 in. to center back at top and taper to ⅝ in. seam at waistline.

Grainline for lining may be straight or bias

Hemline

Hemline

Add ½ in. to finished hemline on back, sleeve, and front.

Back

Sleeve

Front

Key
Original jacket pattern (includes seam allowances)
Removed from pattern
Added to pattern
--- New cutting line

as the jacket pattern, with the exception of the sleeve, which can be cut on either the straight or bias grain. Remove facing width from fronts and back. Add 1¼-in. seam allowances to new line.

Lower the back and front shoulders by one-half the shoulder-pad thickness. The armhole will be smaller once the shoulder pad is in place; if you choose not to adjust here, you'll simply end up with more ease.

Raise the sleeve armholes ½ in. to ⅝ in. from notch to notch. Cut the underarm of the lining body ½ in. to ⅝ in. higher than the jacket pattern from notch to notch. This allows the lining to fit smoothly up and over the upright underarm seam.

Lower the sleeve cap by one-half the shoulder-pad thickness, tapering to notches.

Cut a 1-in. center-back pleat for ease. For a boxy jacket, place the center back of the lining pattern, neck to hem, ¾ in. to 1 in. from the fabric fold when cutting. For jackets with a center-back seam, add 1 in. at the neck and cut parallel to the seam to within 1 in. to 2 in. above the waist, then taper to a regular ⅝-in. seam at the waistline. Eliminate the sleeve vent and follow the underarm-seam cutting line to the hem.

MAKING A PATTERN FOR A PARTIAL LINING

Use front and back interfacing pieces from the figure on page 35 for a base, then raise the underarm ½ in. to ⅝ in., tapering to notch. Lower the back and front shoulders by one-half the shoulder-pad thickness. Cut the sleeves of lining fabric, as described on page 37.

The back and front lining pieces can be cut from lightweight fashion fabric, but it may be best to use regular lining fabric for the back to minimize bulk. If your fashion fabric is too heavy to use for lining the chest and underarm, cut this section from lining fabric.

Use the facing pattern piece as a guide to cut apart the partial lining pattern. Add 1¼ in. to the cutting line of the chest/underarm section so this lining piece can be seamed to the facing.

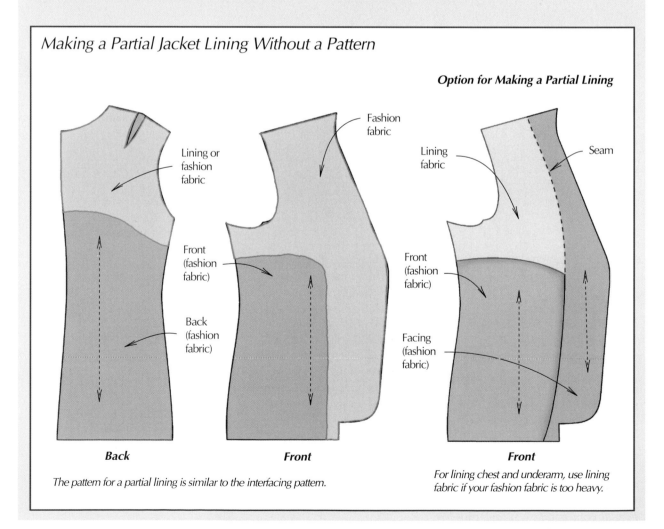

Making a Partial Jacket Lining Without a Pattern

Option for Making a Partial Lining

Lining or fashion fabric

Fashion fabric

Lining fabric

Seam

Front (fashion fabric)

Back (fashion fabric)

Front (fashion fabric)

Facing (fashion fabric)

Back

Front

Front

The pattern for a partial lining is similar to the interfacing pattern.

For lining chest and underarm, use lining fabric if your fashion fabric is too heavy.

Covered Shoulder Pads for Set-in Sleeves Cut a square of lining or lightweight fashion fabric along the straight-of-the-grain, large enough to wrap around the pad and extend ½ in. beyond the outer edges.

Place the pad on the ham to help retain its shape as you cover it. Turn the fabric diagonally to use its flexible bias grain. Wrap the pad's top side loosely, pinning the fabric in place.

Remove the pad from the ham. Keeping it curved, smooth the lining over the underside, pleating as necessary to absorb excess fabric. Take care not to pull tightly. Pin in place.Stitch around the pad, then serge, zigzag, or pink the outer edges. Press the outer edges and flatten pleats.

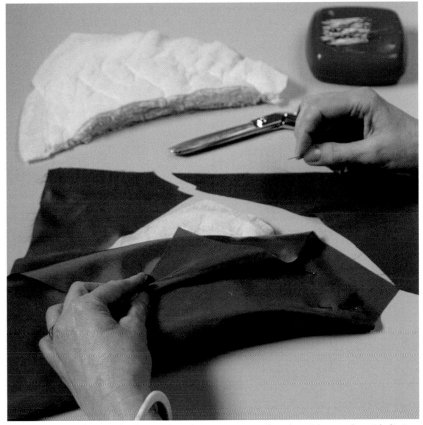

If you plan to line only the jacket sleeves, cover the shoulder pads with lining or lightweight fashion fabric.

Patch Pockets

Patch pockets are designed in a variety of shapes and sizes and can be applied just above or below the jacket waist. Aim for consistency in your jacket's design: Choose larger pockets for large, loose jackets, and smaller ones for smaller, closely fitted styles. Likewise, jackets with curved front edges demand rounded pockets, and squared-off jackets look best with angular pockets.

Draw the shape you want on paper, then place your hand over it to be certain the pocket is large enough to be functional. Pockets below the waist should easily accommodate the width of your hand plus 1 in. to 2 in. of ease, and be deep enough to enclose most of your hand from fingertips to wrist. Be sure square corners are at right angles and curved corners are the same shape on each side.

When pin-fitting your jacket, experiment with the pocket size and placement, then mark the placement on the jacket pattern, leaving ¼ in. ease across the top edge so that the pocket's top edge does not lie completely flat.

Add an extended hem facing of at least 1 in. to the upper edge. The line between the pocket and the hem facing now becomes the fold line. To make a lining pattern, fold the hem facing back over the pocket and trace the remainder of the pocket, from the lower facing edge to the bottom.

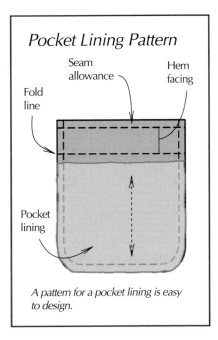

Pocket Lining Pattern

Seam allowance

Hem facing

Fold line

Pocket lining

A pattern for a pocket lining is easy to design.

Add ⅝-in. seam allowances to the lower edge of the facing (for a lined or unlined pocket), the upper edge of the lining, and around the outer edges of the pocket and lining.

Adjusting Sleeve Cap Ease

Take a moment to learn the parts of a set-in sleeve. It's helpful in understanding why seemingly minor adjustments can strongly affect how easily a sleeve can be set into the armhole, and how smooth the cap looks.

Capline: A line drawn from one side to the other at the underarm, dividing the cap from the sleeve body.

Sleeve cap: The sleeve section above the capline ranges in height from around 8 in. for a high-cut, set-in sleeve, to 2 in. or less for a dropped-shoulder sleeve. Thicker shoulder pads require higher sleeve caps, and the cap width must accommodate the arm girth plus 2 in. to 3 in. of ease.

Cap seamline: The stitching line from the front underarm to the top of the sleeve and down to the back underarm. Usually one notch indicates the cap front and two notches indicates the back. The cap seamline from underarm to notch may be ⅛ in. to ¼ in. larger than the underarm of the jacket armhole in front and back, for a total of ½ in. ease. From the notches to the top of the sleeve, the cap seamlines will measure ⅝ in. to 1 in. larger than their respective armhole sections, for a total of 1½ in. to 2 in. of ease.

Sleeve grainline: Placed perpendicular to the capline, this grainline extends from the top of the sleeve to the hem. If sleeve alterations skew the capline and the grainline, redraw a new capline from underarm to underarm, and then place the grainline perpendicular to it.

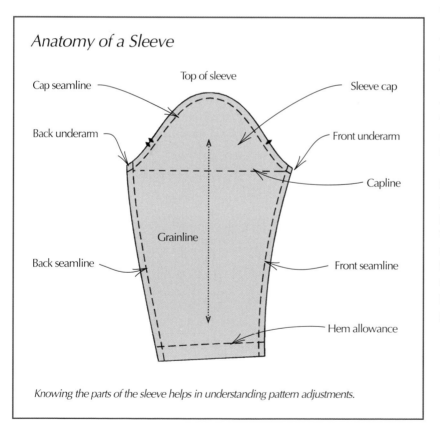

Anatomy of a Sleeve

Cap seamline — Top of sleeve — Sleeve cap

Back underarm — Front underarm

— Capline

Grainline

Back seamline — Front seamline

— Hem allowance

Knowing the parts of the sleeve helps in understanding pattern adjustments.

Reducing Sleeve Cap Ease

For jackets, set-in sleeves are commonly eased into the armhole for a smooth cap. Soft woolens ease beautifully, while polyesters, some blends, and gabardines will be more difficult. If you are unsure of how your fabric will ease, you can cut the sleeve as is and, if necessary, move the seamline in a bit toward the cap as you sew it, tapering in from the sleeve top to notches.

To reduce ease before cutting the sleeve, measure the front and back of the sleeve cap and the armhole with a flexible ruler or a tape measure placed on its side. If your fabric is a difficult-to-ease type, reduce the sleeve cap ease by at least $1/2$ in. An easy way is to place two parallel lines $1/4$ in. apart and at right angles to the grainline, in the upper third of the cap. Fold the lower line up to meet the top line, tape in place, and redraw the cap seamline. The seamline is reduced by $1/2$ in. and the cap height by $1/4$ in. Don't alter any further than this.

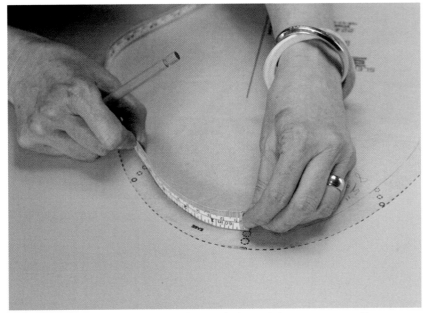

Carefully measure and compare the armhole and sleeve cap seamlines to determine the ease.

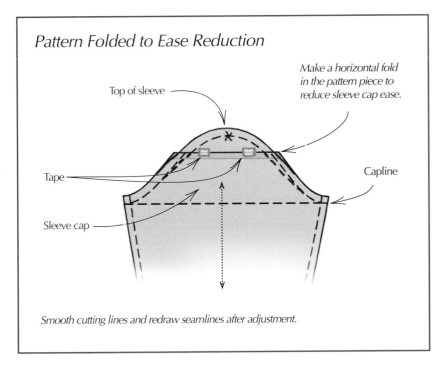

Pattern Folded to Ease Reduction

Top of sleeve

Make a horizontal fold in the pattern piece to reduce sleeve cap ease.

Tape

Capline

Sleeve cap

Smooth cutting lines and redraw seamlines after adjustment.

Cutting and Marking

You have straightened and preshrunk your fabrics and adjusted and refined your pattern. Now it's time to cut and mark your fabrics. The rotary cutter is ideal for cutting jacket fabrics and linings, and dressmaker's weights are a welcome replacement for pins, especially on extremely slippery or heavyweight fabrics.

Lay out the adjusted pattern pieces on the fabric, holding them in place with dressmaker's weights or pins. It's safest to place all pieces in one direction on the fabric, as sometimes a nap doesn't show until the pieces are sewn together. Measure each pattern piece from its grainline arrow to the fabric selvage (do this in several places along the grainline arrow) to ensure that it is on grain.

With tailor's chalk, mark any additional pattern revisions, such as widening seam allowances or raising a lining underarm, directly on the fabric (1).

Once all pattern pieces are in place, begin cutting. Using the rotary cutter, follow the pattern cutting lines (2). Don't stop for notches and other markings—cut straight across them. To add seam allowance width as you cut, place a clear gridded ruler at the pattern edge, and cut.

When working with a fabric that looks the same on both sides, stick a piece of tape to the right side for easy identification.

Mark each piece as soon as you cut it. Always mark on the wrong side of the fabric. I prefer to snip-mark or trace with dressmaker's tracing paper and a wheel. To snip-mark the center front, center back, notches, dots, dart ends, and any other marks around the pattern edges, snip ⅛ in. into the seam allowance with scissors (**3**). Mark inner details such as darts and pockets with a tracing wheel (**4**). If your fabric is too textured to work properly with the tracing paper, push a pin through each marking, then chalk-mark the pin position on the fabric's wrong side.

Using a gridded ruler with one metal edge keeps you from slicing into the plastic and dulling the cutting blade.

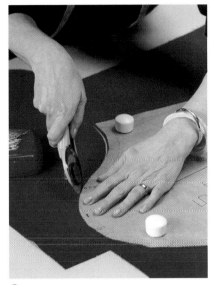

1 *Chalk-mark a wider seam allowance directly on the fabric.*

2 *Rotary-cut over notches, then snip to mark their placement afterward.*

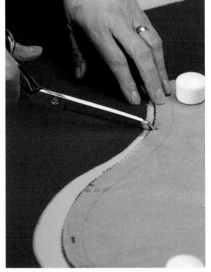

3 *Snip notches while pattern is in place over the fabric.*

4 *Mark your fabric with a tracing wheel; preserve your pattern tissue by placing a piece of clear plastic between the tracing wheel and the pattern.*

4 The Best Sewing Techniques

Now you're ready for the fun part: putting the pieces together. In the following pages, detailed instructions, photos, and drawings guide you through all aspects of assembling your jacket. This is where I reorganize my project according to the process method, completing all like tasks at one time, and I substitute fast-and-easy sewing-industry techniques wherever possible. Before you begin, review the sewing order and the techniques that I suggest in this chapter and compare them to those on your pattern guide sheet. Reorganize and mark up your guide sheet so that the steps will be clear as you put your jacket together. For examples throughout I use a cardigan jacket, since this is by far the most popular style.

Knowing why you do something is almost as important as the task itself. With this in mind, I describe the principles behind the basic techniques. Optional techniques—those things that are nice to know but not essential—are highlighted for easy reference, and the chapter is rounded out with tips for troubleshooting and emulating the ready-to-wear industry.

A substantial portion of this chapter is devoted to traditional pressing techniques used by tailors, because these methods are crucial for a contemporary tailored jacket. Your jacket should have crisp edges, well-shaped sleeve caps, and fabric that looks newly purchased. This finished look is acquired only through proper—and frequent—pressing. Use the appropriate pressing tools, and practice on fabric samples to learn pressing techniques and to avoid a puffy, underpressed look or shiny, flattened surfaces.

Many of the sewing techniques illustrated here are used in better jacket factories to produce a high-quality product in the shortest possible time. It makes sense for home sewers to try to do the same. You'll be pleased with the results and how easy they are to obtain.

Before You Sew

Following are the steps for assembling lined, partially lined, or unlined jackets using the process method. Think of your jacket in terms of individual units (the fronts, back, pockets, sleeves, facings, and lining), and work on several units at a time.

Fully Lined Jackets

1. Straighten the grain and preshrink (page 17) the fashion, lining, and interfacing fabrics.

2. Pin-fit and alter the pattern (pages 26-33), making sure the same changes are made to pieces that will be seamed together and to corresponding lining pieces.

3. Refine the pattern pieces for any changes, such as:
• increasing the hem depth (page 28)
• widening or narrowing seam allowances (page 28)
• redesigning interfacing shapes (pages 34-36)
• bagging the lining (pages 36-39)
• changing pocket style or placement (pages 39-40)
• simplifying the sleeve vent (pages 79-81)
• adjusting the sleeve cap ease (pages 40-41)

4. Cut and mark all fabrics (pages 42-43), leaving inner-jacket markings (with the exception of darts) to be transferred after interfacing is applied.

5. Fuse interfacing to all pieces, using the flat or finished-edge method (pages 63-65).

6. Mark all inner-jacket details after fusing the interfacing.

7. Sew and press the following:
• darts (page 60)
• pockets (pages 66-68)
• front and back facings (page 73)
• sleeve-vent seam (page 81)
• lining, leaving one sleeve seam partially open (pages 96-97)

8. Press sleeve hems in place (page 79).

9. Complete the pockets and sew them to the jacket fronts (pages 67-69), or baste them if you are unsure of the placement; topstitch or edgestitch if desired.

10. Join the front to the back at the shoulder seams, stabilizing with tape if necessary; staystitch and clip the neck edge. If you are unsure about how the front and back will fit you, baste them together for now.

Possible Revisions in Jacket Construction

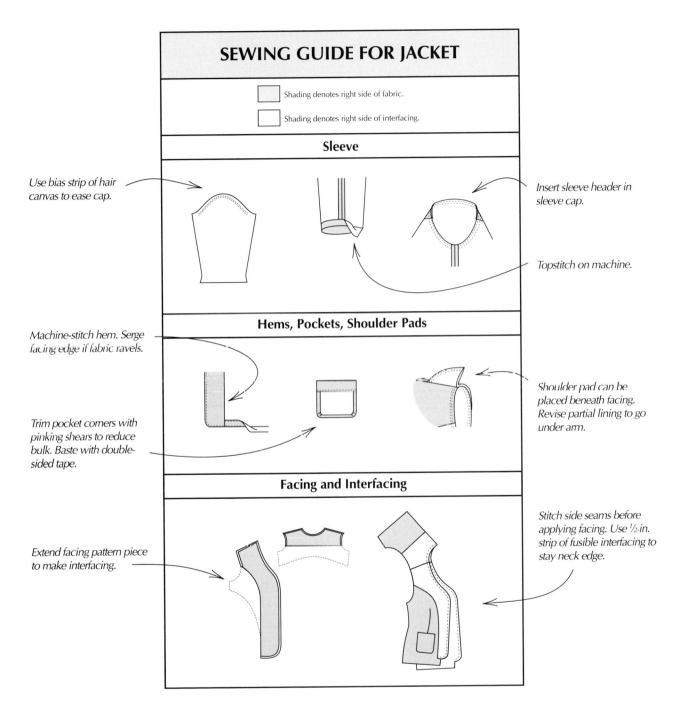

SEWING GUIDE FOR JACKET

Shading denotes right side of fabric.

Shading denotes right side of interfacing.

Sleeve

Use bias strip of hair canvas to ease cap.

Insert sleeve header in sleeve cap.

Topstitch on machine.

Hems, Pockets, Shoulder Pads

Machine-stitch hem. Serge facing edge if fabric ravels.

Trim pocket corners with pinking shears to reduce bulk. Baste with double-sided tape.

Shoulder pad can be placed beneath facing. Revise partial lining to go under arm.

Facing and Interfacing

Extend facing pattern piece to make interfacing.

Stitch side seams before applying facing. Use ½-in. strip of fusible interfacing to stay neck edge.

There are many changes a sewer can make to a pattern company's suggested sewing guide. The example above illustrates just a few.

11. Machine-baste the side seams, and fit the jacket before final stitching and pressing (pages 70-71).

12. Sew the facing unit to the jacket, taping the front opening and neckline, and press and grade the seam allowances (pages 72-75).

13. Hem the jacket body in the center of the hem allowance, to prepare for bagging the lining (pages 76-77).

14. Complete the sleeves (pages 82-84): Sew the remaining sleeve seam, hem the sleeves in the center of the hem allowance, then ease the sleeve cap and press the seam allowance.

15. Stitch the sleeves into the jacket (pages 85-87). Finger-press the sleeve cap, and insert a sleeve header if needed (page 88).

16. Insert the shoulder pads and lightly tack down the facings at the shoulder and chest areas (page 89).

17. Work any topstitching or edgestitching (page 51).

18. Final press before lining (page 59).

19. Bag the lining (pages 97-105).

20. Machine-stitch buttonholes and sew on buttons (pages 107-108).

Partially Lined Jackets

1. Follow steps 1 through 11 and 14 through 16, preceding.

2. Join the underarm of the front and back facings. Finish exposed inner edges of facings.

3. Insert the sleeve lining into the facing armhole (page 106). Follow step 12 in preceding list and step 4 in section below .

4. Sew the lining to the jacket-sleeve hems (page 106).

5. Machine-stitch buttonholes and sew on buttons (pages 107-108).

Unlined Jackets

If you plan to line only the sleeves, refer to pages 105-106.

1. Follow steps 1 through 11 for fully lined jackets, ignoring all lining references.

2. Finish the side and shoulder-seam edges (page 105).

3. Finish the inner edge of facing unit, and sew facing to jacket. Follow step 12 for fully lined jackets.

4. Finish the top edge of the hem and stitch it in place (page 105).

5. Follow steps 14 through 17 and step 20 for fully lined jackets, using covered shoulder pads. Finish top edge of sleeve hems and stitch in place.

Stitches, Seams, and Finishes

The techniques presented here complement easy jackets. Some may be new to you, such as the square-corner method borrowed from the garment industry; others you may recognize, such as the catchstitch, a holdover from traditional tailoring. It's the combination of hand- and machine-sewing that gives your jacket a fine finish.

Hand Stitches

Using hand stitches is where the home-sewn jacket surpasses the ready-to-wear garment. Hand stitching is used only for finishing—in hems, buttons, and shoulder pads—but it is vitally important. For example, the ready-to-wear industry usually leaves jacket hems unstitched, relying on the lining or small bits of fusible web to hold the hem in place. The hand catchstitch gives a much nicer finish, and there is no chance of the hem folding down beyond the crease line.

To make thread more durable, pull it through beeswax after threading the needle, then pull the thread across your fingernail to remove excess wax.

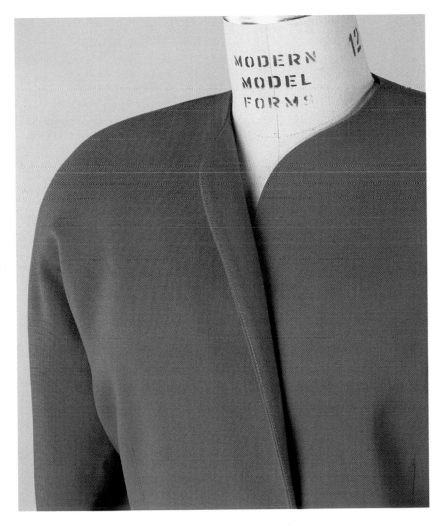

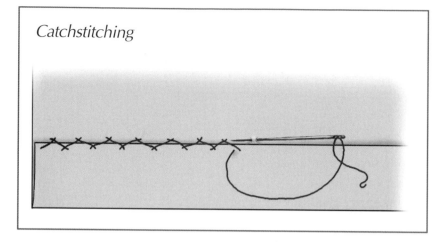

Catchstitching

Catchstitch The catchstitch is a traditional tailor's stitch used for many applications, including inconspicuous hems. With a single thread, work from left to right, catching a yarn of the jacket fabric with a horizontal stitch. Move the needle down to the hem, at least ¹/₂ in. from the first stitch, and take a second horizontal stitch, again catching only one yarn. The thread crosses after each horizontal stitch, and stitches are quite loose for flexibility.

Permanent Basting In places where machine stitching can't reach or would be too rigid, such as sleeve headers and shoulder pads, use permanent basting. Take ¹/₄-in. to ¹/₂-in. stitches with one or two strands of beeswaxed thread, pulling stitches apart every 2 in. to 3 in. to keep them loose and to allow the fabrics to move.

Stab Stitch When horizontal stitches are impossible, the stab stitch will hold bulky fabrics or shoulder pads securely. Using a doubled beeswaxed thread, stab the needle into the fabric, pull it to the other side, and stab it back into the fabric at nearly the same spot it came from. Keep the stitches loose to prevent dimples.

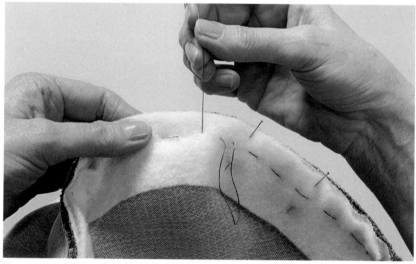

Permanent basting keeps sleeve headers secure while allowing them to move.

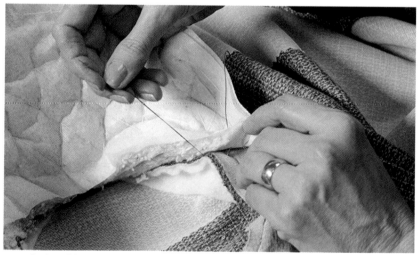

Attach shoulder pads with the stab stitch.

Machine Stitches

Machine Basting Used in place of hand-basting, machine-basting is a long machine stitch (six stitches per inch or fewer) that holds fabrics together temporarily and is easily pulled out. Use it for joining seams for fitting, easing sleeve caps, and basting the center-back lining pleat for pressing. Some machines have an extra-long basting stitch that is particularly good for linings, since it leaves fewer needle holes.

Edgestitching and Topstitching If you perfect edgestitching and topstitching, your work will rival better quality ready-to-wear jackets. Both stitches are regular straight machine stitches. Edgestitching is placed along open edges to hold them flat, or along the wells of seams or darts for accent. Topstitching is placed at least ¼ in. away from edgestitching, open edges, or the wells of seams and darts, and is decorative as well as functional.

To topstitch, align the inner edge of the presser foot or special topstitching foot with the fabric edge or the seam well, and change the needle position. Perfectly straight stitching is easier with the Straight Tape notion (see page 23). Place tape on the fabric as a sewing guide.

Edgestitch slightly away from the edge, parallel to the topstitching line, and watch the guide—not the needle—as you stitch. Sew slowly for straighter lines, and take curves slower still; pivot at corners. At the end, backstitch or leave enough thread to draw through to the back and tie off.

Using Straight Tape can enable you to sew a perfectly straight line of topstitching, following a line of edgestitching underneath the tape.

Experiment with various stitch lengths and threads before you apply any stitching to your jacket. A longer stitch length (eight to ten stitches per inch) shows up nicely on jacket-weight fabrics. Use topstitching thread or buttonhole twist with a topstitching or #16 needle.

Staystitching Staystitching is a regular straight stitch that keeps curved areas, such as neck edges, from stretching, and reinforces seam allowances or corners that will be straightened by clipping. Place stitches ⅛ in. from the seamline in the seam allowance. When reinforcing corners, use smaller stitches and sew directly on the seamline so the clipped corner will be secured when attaching a second piece.

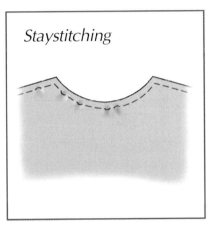

Staystitching

Stitch in the Ditch A fast technique often found in ready-to-wear garments, stitching in the ditch replaces more time-consuming hand sewing. Regular length or slightly longer machine stitches are applied along the well of a seam, or "in the ditch." It is often used in inconspicuous areas to hold facings in place. Closely match your thread to the fabric, in case your stitches are not exactly in the well of the seam.

Understitching A regular straight stitch to hold seam allowances to facing edges to keep facings from rolling outside, understitching gives a jacket a sharp edge. Before understitching, press open and grade the seam allowances so that the garment's is wider than the facing's. Top-press them in one direction from the right side of the facing. Stitch from the right side of the facing, close to the seam, making sure both seam allowances are caught in the stitching.

Seams and Finishes

Plain Seam, Unfinished A plain seam is the most basic seam and is best used in firmly woven fabrics and fully lined jackets. With right sides together, straight-stitch the seam, then press open. Most plain seams are ⅝ in. wide, but 1-in. wide seams press and lie flatter in wools, especially in vertical and shoulder seams.

Plain Seam, Finished with Serging, Binding, or Zigzagging With a finished edge, a plain ⅝-in. wide seam is suitable for unlined or partially lined jackets. The edge treatment is personal preference: A bound edge is more luxurious, but serging and zigzagging both produce durable, fast finishes. For loosely woven fabrics, consider serging or zigzagging the edges even if the jacket will be lined.

Serged Seam Stitched and overlocked at the same time, a serged seam should be used only for lightweight, unlined, casual jackets. Serged seams cannot be pressed open before being pressed to one side and are too bulky for a smooth finish. Rather than a serged seam, use a plain seam with each edge serged individually, then held in place with edgestitching or topstitching.

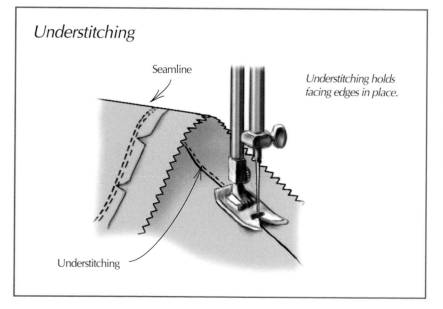

Understitching

Seamline

Understitching holds facing edges in place.

Understitching

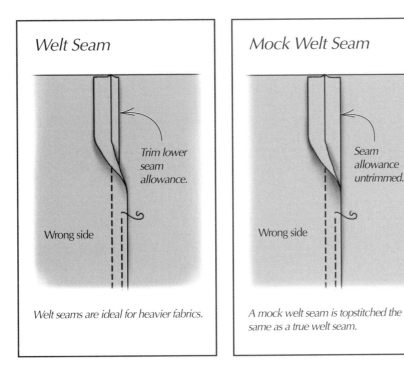

Welt Seam

Trim lower seam allowance.

Wrong side

Welt seams are ideal for heavier fabrics.

Mock Welt Seam

Seam allowance untrimmed.

Wrong side

A mock welt seam is topstitched the same as a true welt seam.

Welt Seam The hallmark of a welt seam is a ridge (or welt) defined by topstitching on the fabric's right side. This seam is useful for lined or unlined jackets and quite practical for medium- to heavyweight fabrics. Begin with a plain seam; press seam allowances open and then both in one direction (usually toward the back). Trim the lower seam allowance just short of topstitching width. If the jacket is unlined, serge or zigzag the upper seam allowance. Topstitch the seam from the right side, pinning the allowance as necessary to prevent it from stretching as you sew. If it does stretch, stop stitching every few inches, leaving the needle in the fabric. Raise the presser foot and smooth fabric toward the back. If the topstitching is to be wider than $1/4$ in., cut wider seam allowances to begin with.

Mock Welt Seam From the right side, the mock welt seam looks like a welt seam because it is topstitched, but there is no welt. It is a quick alternative to a true welt seam, and can be used on light- to medium-weight fabrics, especially in unlined or partially lined jackets. Begin with a $5/8$-in. plain seam. Press allowances open and then to one side, usually toward the back of the jacket. Serge both seam edges (together or separately), and topstitch from the right side.

Use a 6-in. seam gauge to hold the fabric smooth in front of the needle, pushing it slightly as the feed dogs move the fabric along.

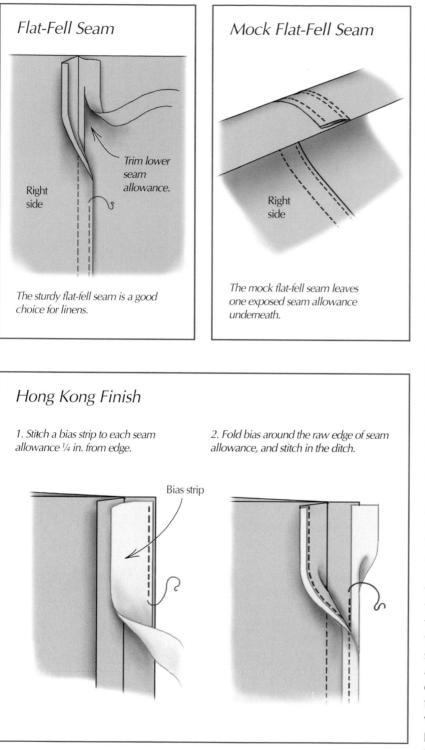

Flat-Fell Seam

The sturdy flat-fell seam is a good choice for linens.

Right side

Trim lower seam allowance.

Mock Flat-Fell Seam

The mock flat-fell seam leaves one exposed seam allowance underneath.

Right side

Hong Kong Finish

1. Stitch a bias strip to each seam allowance ¼ in. from edge.

2. Fold bias around the raw edge of seam allowance, and stitch in the ditch.

Bias strip

Flat-Fell Seam The flat-fell seam is identified by its two parallel rows of topstitching. It is sturdy and works well with lightweight, firmly woven fabrics that press easily, such as linens. It is especially good for unlined or partially lined jackets. Begin with a plain ⅝-in. seam, but place wrong sides together. Press seam allowances open and then in the direction you want the seam to fall, usually toward the back. Trim the lower seam allowance to ¼ in. Fold the raw edge of the upper seam allowance around the trimmed edge, press in place, and edgestitch along this folded edge (double-sided basting tape holds it down well).

Mock Flat-Fell Seam Sew and press a plain seam as for the mock welt, except from the right side edgestitch close to the seam well, then topstitch ¼ in. away from the edgestitching. On the right side this looks like a flat-fell seam, but on the wrong side it has one exposed seam allowance.

Hong Kong Finish The Hong Kong finish is an elegant binding for facing edges, seam allowances, and hems in unlined or partially lined jackets. From lining fabric that coordinates with the fashion fabric, cut 1¼-in. wide bias strips that are twice as long as the seam you are finishing. Stitch the bias strips to the right side of each seam allowance, ⅛ in. to ¼ in. from the edge (use ¼ in. for loosely woven fabrics; ⅛ in. for more firmly woven fabrics). Set the stitching, press bias away from seam allowance, then fold and press bias around the raw edge of the seam allowance. Stitch in the ditch to hold the bias in place. Bias-cut fabrics do not ravel, so you can trim any excess binding to ¼ in.

PERFECTING THE HONG KONG FINISH

If your jacket will be unlined or partially lined, finished (Hong Kong) seams will both protect the seams from fraying and give the jacket interior a look of professional tailoring.

To Cut Bias Strips

Starting with at least ½ yard of fabric, fold the fabric diagonally so the crosswise grain aligns with the selvage. Press then cut along the fold. The cut edge is the true bias. Align a clear gridded ruler to the cut edge, and cut strips to the desired width using a rotary cutter. To join end on end, align strips at right angles to form a V. Stitch ¼-in. seams, and press open.

To Finish Seams

To finish the seams, sew 1¼-in. strips of lining or other fabric cut on the bias to the seam allowance edge (1), right sides together. Turn fabric back, and press (2)

Fold the bias fabric under the seam, and press (3). Topstitch the bias fabric to the seam allowance (4).

Trim any excess bias fabric from underside of seam allowance (5). This provides a finished and professional appearance to seams that will show inside the jacket.

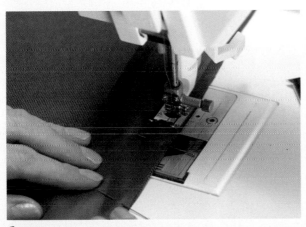

1 *Pin and sew strips of bias-cut fabric to seam allowance, right sides together.*

2 *Turn bias strip and press.*

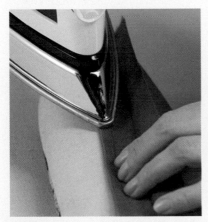

3 *Fold under the bias fabric, and press.*

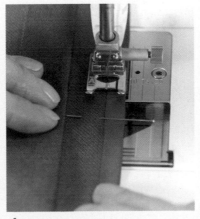

4 *Topstitch the bias fabric to the seam allowance.*

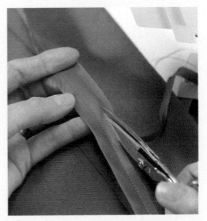

5 *Trim any excess bias fabric from underside of seam allowance.*

Pressing Fundamentals

Construction pressing may actually take longer than the sewing process, but the results are well worth the time. If you emulate the pressing guidelines of professional tailors, your jacket will have sharp edges, flat seams and darts, stable facings, and well-shaped sleeve caps.

Depending on the fabric, the amount of heat, moisture, and pressure used in pressing vary. Pressing is different from ironing, because you raise and lower the iron on and off the fabric (you do not use a gliding, side-to-side motion) to prevent stretching.

Before you work on a piece of your garment, press a 6-in. long test seam to see if the fabric water spots, changes color, or loses its shape or surface texture. Examine the fabric carefully. If there are changes, modify your pressing procedure and test again, adjusting the heat, moisture, pressure, and press cloth until the result is satisfactory.

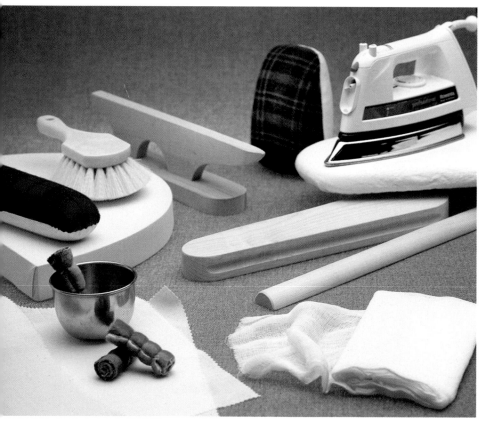

Essential Pressing Equipment

- Steam/dry iron (preferably heavyweight)
- Padded ironing board or table
- Seam roll and/or wooden Seam Stick press bar
- Tailor's ham
- Point presser
- Wooden clapper
- Tailor's cheese block
- Tailor's dauber or sponge
- Woven press cloths (two lightweight and see-through; one heavyweight muslin, duck, or self-fabric)
- Cheesecloth
- Tailor's or clothes brush

Construction Pressing

In construction pressing, we put moisture into the fabric and then dry it thoroughly before moving it. Pressing wool, a favorite jacket fabric, is tricky. Once you can press wool, other fibers are easy. Wool absorbs and retains a lot of moisture. If wool remains damp after pressing, it will dry on its own and "spring back to life." Seams and darts that you thought were pressed will be puffy and unpressed. Here's how to avoid such pitfalls.

Setting the Stitch After stitching, seams and darts may be rippled or puckered. Press along the stitched area on the wrong side with a steam iron. This forces the machine stitches to meld with the woven yarns, and thus sets the stitch. Switch the iron to the dry setting and repeat the process to begin drying the fabric.

Experiment with the amount of moisture you use on each fabric. You don't want to soak the spot, yet you will probably need more dampness than the iron alone provides.

MAKING A TAILOR'S DAUBER AND CHEESE BLOCK

In pressing wool, the dauber and cheese block are invaluable. To make a tailor's dauber, roll a 3-in. wide strip of firmly woven, colorfast wool (such as flannel) into a 1-in. diameter cylinder. Wrap and tightly tie the center and ends with sewing thread. When pressing, wet the end of the dauber to apply moisture to a specific part of the garment.

A cheese block enables you to get flat, sharp edges. Cut the cheese block from hardwood such as maple or birch, according to the dimensions shown. (Hardwood is a must; if softer woods are used, heat from the iron may draw sap to the pressing surface and damage your fabric.) If you like, cover it with muslin. I usually stretch two layers of muslin tightly across the board, then tack them underneath with a staple gun. Keep the muslin smooth, especially across the top of the curve.

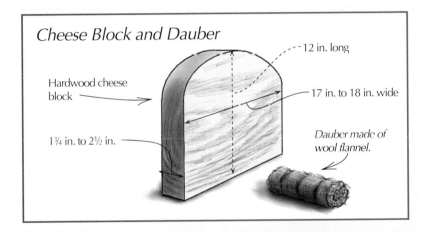

Cheese Block and Dauber

- 12 in. long
- Hardwood cheese block
- 17 in. to 18 in. wide
- 1¾ in. to 2½ in.
- *Dauber made of wool flannel.*

Set the stitch to remove ripples or puckers.

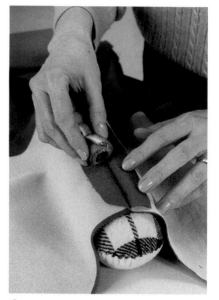

1 *Apply moisture with the tailor's dauber.*

2 *Under-press the seam.*

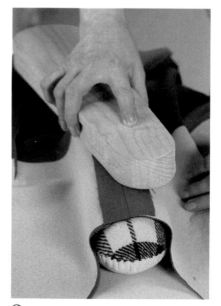

3 *Clap or pat the seam to dry.*

4 *Always use a press cloth for top-pressing.*

Under-Pressing Pressing from the wrong side of the fabric requires no press cloth. Use the dauber on wool to apply moisture directly to the fabric; for other fibers, use the iron itself to apply moisture.

Place the seam over a seam roll (to keep cut edges from making an impression in the fabric). Use the dauber to apply a bead of moisture along the stitched area (1).

Press the seam with a dry iron, using a raising-and-lowering motion, and apply pressure where the iron touches the fabric (2).

Strike with a wooden clapper or pat with your hand to aid drying. Work in sections along the length of the seam roll, and be sure each section is almost dry before moving on (3).

Top-Pressing Although your results so far may look wonderful, don't skip top-pressing. Pressing the right side of the fabric further improves your jacket's final appearance.

Always use a press cloth when you press a fabric's right side (4). For wool, use a heavyweight cotton duck press cloth that has been chemically treated to prevent shine. If your test seam reveals a shiny surface texture, test again with a piece of the fashion fabric

Use a Seam Stick press bar when working with fabrics, such as gabardine, that have high-twist yarns and resist pressing. The hardwood stick gives a seam a much sharper press than the softer seam roll.

between the test fabric's right side and the press cloth. For fabrics other than wool, use a transparent, lightweight press cloth.

To top-press a seam, place the seam roll or Seam Stick press bar beneath it. Place a small bead of moisture on the press cloth using the dauber, and press with a dry iron.

Off-Pressing Off-pressing is necessary only if the fabric's surface texture has flattened or become shiny from other pressing. Dip a piece of cheesecloth in water, wring it out, and place it over the flattened fabric. Hold the iron so it just touches the cheesecloth (photo below). This forces steam into the fabric and raises its surface texture. Don't place the weight of the iron directly onto the fabric. Remove the cheesecloth and pat the surface with an up-and-down hand motion or a tailor's brush.

Final Pressing Once your jacket is assembled and ready to be lined, you may want to top-press lightly with a press cloth. This final touch-up requires little time if you pressed as you went along, but doing it is important.

Moisture from the iron's own spray mist or steam surge is useful when pressing fabrics other than wool. The dauber works best for wool, because the spray mist dampens too great a swath, and the steam surge doesn't impart enough moisture for a crisp, professional finish.

For off-pressing, hold the iron over the damp cheesecloth to allow heat to penetrate into the fabric, in order to raise its surface texture.

Pressing Perfect Darts

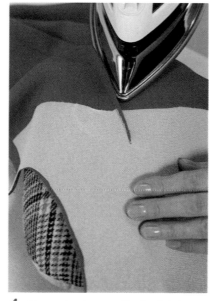

1 *"Kill" the edge of the dart.*

2 *Strike the dart with a clapper to further flatten and dry it.*

3 *Shape the dart on a tailor's ham.*

4 *Use a dry iron to lift the fabric texture and remove the impression of the dart.*

The bulk within darts makes it hard to obtain a smooth tip and a sharp outer crease. These pointers will help you achieve dart perfection.

When setting dart stitching, do not press beyond the stitching at the tip of the dart, since this area is easily stretched.

Flatten or "kill" the dart's folded edge within the stitching line (**1**). Place the dart on the cheeseblock, moisten the fold with the dauber, and press with a dry iron, applying pressure. Strike the dart with the clapper to further flatten and dry it (**2**).

Press the dart with the tip placed on the curve of a tailor's ham (**3**). Again moisten the stitching with the dauber. Press the dart bulk away from you with a dry iron, gently pulling the fabric apart at the stitching line as you press. Lightly moisten below the tip of the dart, and press to shrink and shape around this area.

Darts in bulky, firmly woven fabric may need extra help to flatten. Slash and press the dart fold open to within 1/2 in. of the dart tip. Press the tip to one side.

Top-press using a press cloth. If the dart bulk has left an impression on the right side of the fabric, turn the dart back to the wrong side and moisten this line. Use a dry iron to lift the fabric texture and remove the impression (**4**).

Edges, Corners, and Points

Here are some special techniques for minimizing bulk and producing flawless corners and points. In addition to giving your jacket a more polished final appearance, these methods are helpful for almost any kind of sewing.

Grade enclosed facing seam allowances to minimize bulk.

Grading Seam Allowances

To minimize bulk in enclosed facing seams and hem allowances, trim the seam allowances to different widths (called grading). The widest seam, trimmed to $3/8$ in., is closest to the jacket. The narrowest seam, trimmed to $1/4$ in., is the one closest to the body. If you trim seam allowances any narrower, you may weaken the stitching line and cause a ridge on the right side.

Turn of the Cloth

When two pieces of fabric are seamed, layered, then folded over one another, as in facings and pockets, the top fabric automatically rolls under $1/16$ in. to $1/8$ in. or more. This amount is the turn of the cloth. To compensate, the top layer must be slightly larger than the bottom layer so the seamed piece can lie flat with the seamline rolling slightly under (an indicator of quality construction). Sometimes extra fabric is allowed for the turn; other times it is controlled by pressing the edge.

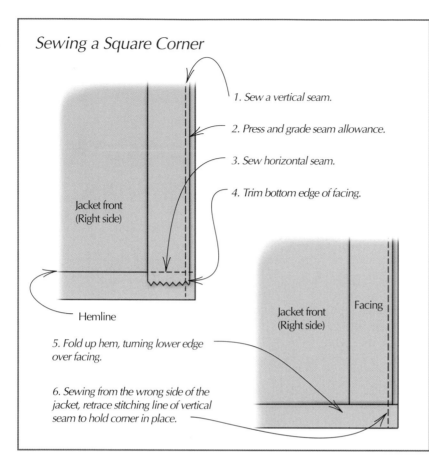

Sewing a Square Corner

Jacket front
(Right side)

1. Sew a vertical seam.

2. Press and grade seam allowance.

3. Sew horizontal seam.

4. Trim bottom edge of facing.

Hemline

5. Fold up hem, turning lower edge over facing.

6. Sewing from the wrong side of the jacket, retrace stitching line of vertical seam to hold corner in place.

Jacket front
(Right side)

Facing

Sewing Square Corners

Square corners are a hallmark of a professionally made garment. Here is an easy industry technique to sew corners that are perfectly square. Use this method wherever two seam allowances cross at right angles, and especially at squared-off lower front jacket edges: Stitch the vertical seam to end or pivot, and stitch to inner edge of facing. Press and grade allowances. Stitch the horizontal seam. Trim bottom edge of facing. Turn the horizontal seam allowance back over the facing. Retrace the stitching line of the vertical seam to hold the corner in place. Do not trim this corner; turn and push it out with a point turner. Give the corner a final pressing from the facing and right sides of the jacket.

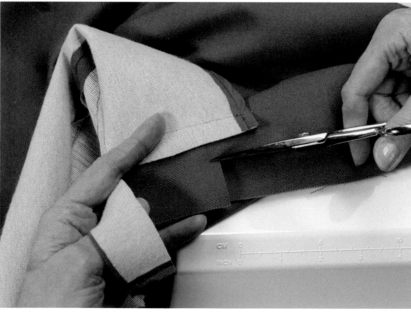

Trim bottom edge of facing and corner fabric.

For a corner to open into straight lines and be integrated into a straight piece of fabric, it must usually be clipped. Reinforce the corner with lightweight fusible tricot, and staystitch on the stitching line for about 1 in. on either side of the corner point. If fabric ravels easily, put a drop of Fray Check adhesive in the corner point. Clip diagonally into the seam allowance.

Applying Interfacings

It's easy to fuse interfacings flawlessly. Remember that the wrong side of fusible interfacing is the side with resin on it. You may need to look closely to detect the resin, since it isn't always obvious.

Interfacing Finishes

When using fusible interfacing, choose one of the methods discussed below.

Flat-Finish Method Garment manufacturers use the flat-finish method frequently, and pattern companies suggest it for fully lined jackets.

Place the interfacing with the resin side against the wrong side of the jacket fabric. Fuse as explained on page 65, using a tabletop press, as shown in photo on right, or an iron.

Finished-Edge Method The inner edges of the facings must be finished for unlined and partially lined jackets. The finished-edge method is ideal for these styles; inner seam allowances are concealed, so no binding, serging, or zigzagging is required.

Place the right side of the interfacing to the right side of the

Since pressure is automatically applied to the fabric, the tabletop press is excellent for fusing. Make sure that any fabric section beneath the heating plate is completely covered with a press cloth.

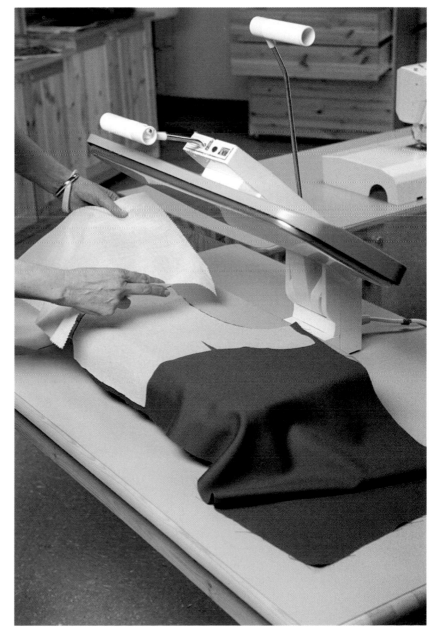

1 With right sides together, sew the interfacing to the facing.

2 Understitch the interfacing to the seam allowance.

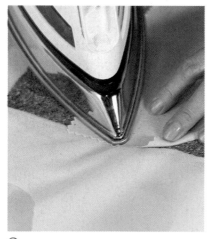

3 Fuse the seam allowance with a press cloth.

4 Steam-baste with the tip of the iron, then fuse.

Don't fuse over seams that are already stitched and pressed open; the seam edges will leave ridges on the jacket's right side.

jacket facing fabric, and make a $\frac{1}{4}$-in. seam along the curved edge to stitch the two pieces together. Clip seams so they will lie flat when turned right side out (1).

Turn, finger-press, and then understitch the interfacing to the seam allowance (2). This stitching will smooth and hold the inner edge flat while you fuse. Fuse the depth of the seam allowance first in order to control the large piece of interfacing and keep it wrinkle-free (3).

Smooth the remaining interfacing, steam-baste the corners in place. Complete the fusing process as explained on page 65. To steam-baste, set the tip of the iron directly on the interfacing and lightly fuse in place (4).

If you must use sew-in interfacing, attach it at the seams, $\frac{1}{2}$ in. from the cut edges.

The Fusing Process

Whether you use the flat method or finished-edge method, general fusing directions are the same. These steps can be used for most interfacings, but always check the directions that come with your interfacing. Some manufacturers suggest a lower iron temperature and a dry iron.

Before fusing, soften the interfacing's inside edges with pinking shears or a rotary cutter that cuts scallops or pinked edges. This keeps the interfacing edges from creating ridges on the fabric's right side when fused.

Set the iron to the wool/steam setting. Lay out the fashion fabric, wrong side up, making sure fabric grain is not skewed. Press the fabric to warm it. Place the interfacing on the fabric, wrong sides together. Be sure the interfacing's resin side is facedown.

Cover the fabric with a transparent press cloth dampened with a spray mister, lower the iron into position, and press for 10 to 12 seconds (1). The lightweight press cloth allows you to see through and check for wrinkles in the interfacing placement. Put pressure on the iron as you press; if necessary, lower the ironing board so you can press harder.

To fuse the next part of the interfacing, lift, move, and lower the iron into position, liberally overlapping the first part to make sure the bond is complete. Do not slide the iron, since the interfacing will become distorted. Mist the press cloth each time you move to a new place (2). Continue in this fashion until you've fused the entire interfacing piece.

Turn the fabric section over to the right side and repeat steps 1 and 2, using a heavy-duty press cloth.

Keep resin on interfacing in its place: An opaque Teflon press sheet will keep excess resin off the ironing board, and using one press cloth for fusing on the wrong side and another for final pressing on the right side will prevent resin transfer to the fabric's right side.

1 *As you press, look through the press cloth for wrinkles.*

2 *Use a plant mister to dampen the press cloth. It gives better coverage than the spray iron. Mist the press cloth each time you move to a new place.*

Patch Pockets

Pockets may be lined or unlined, but they should always be interfaced, so that the outer fabric has the support it needs for appearance and durability. It's easiest to finish pockets and attach them to the jacket before you join the front pieces at the shoulder and side seams.

Sewing Lined Pockets

As does an unlined patch pocket, a lined patch pocket needs a hem facing to finish and support its upper edge.

Join the lining to the pocket by stitching completely across the upper edge with right sides together. Press both seam allowances toward the lining. Turn the pocket to the wrong side along the hem-facing fold.

Trim ⅛ in. from the lining, tapering from the upper seam (**1**). Match, pin, and sew the cut edges of the lining and pocket, decreasing stitch length around the curves to keep them smooth. If the pocket has square corners at the lower edge, stitch the lower seam before sewing the sides, remembering to leave about 2 in. open in the center. Sew the corners by folding the bottom seam up over the vertical seams and retracing the stitching (see Sewing Square Corners, page 62).

Set the stitch and press the lining seam allowance in toward the pocket center. Grade the seam allowances with pinking shears on the curves (**2**), then turn the pocket

Sewing Lined Pockets

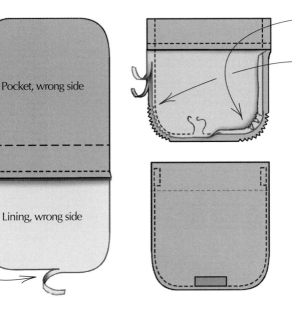

Construction

1. Stitch top edges. Leave 2-in. to 3-in. opening in bottom seam.

2. Press seam allowances toward lining.

3. Trim ⅛ in. from lining before stitching to pocket, tapering to meet stitching at top edge.

4. Stitch pocket to lining, matching cut edges.

5. Press lining seam allowance toward pocket.

6. Grade lining seam allowance to ¼ in. and pocket to ⅜ in.; pink curves.

7. Turn right side out through opening. Press. Seam will roll toward smaller lining.

Finishing Details

8. Close opening with fusible web inserted into opening and press. Topstitch across lower edge of interfacing.

9. Edgestitch pocket to jacket, reinforcing top corners with rectangles.

Pocket, wrong side

Lining, wrong side

1 Trim ⅛ in. off the lining.

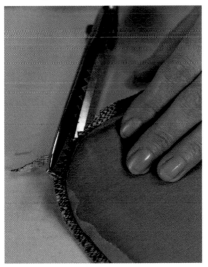

2 Use pinking shears to trim the curved edge of the pocket to reduce bulk.

It's easier to sew identical curves if you approach each curve from the same direction. Begin at the upper right with the jacket fabric next to the feed dogs, and sew to within 1 in. of the bottom center. Then turn the pocket over and again stitch from the upper right to within 1 in. of the bottom center. Leave the opening wider for heavier fabrics.

through the opening in the bottom seam. Use a point turner for sharp, square corners.

Because the lining was cut smaller, the upper fabric will roll to the underside even without pressing.

Press on a cheese block from the lining side to make sure the fabric rolls under evenly around the entire pocket. Close the opening in the lower edge with a narrow strip of fusible web, or close it when the pocket is stitched to the jacket.

SEWING CURVED POCKET EDGES

On top of the cheese block, trim the remaining unpressed seam allowances to ⅜ in. with pinking shears, simultaneously notching the curves and finishing the raw edges, or use a serger to finish the seam edges. Set the curves with a steam iron, using a metal pocket template for shaping **(1)**.

Still using the cheese block, match one of the template corners to your pocket corner, placing the template ⅜ in. from the cut edge. With a steam iron, press the fabric edge over the template and then place the clamp over this edge to hold the seam in place **(2)**.

Press the remaining straight edges under ⅜ in. to align with the corners and the finished upper edge. If your fabric is wool, switch the iron to the dry setting and set the crease with the clapper before removing the clamp **(3)**.

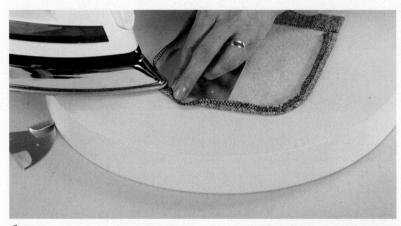

1 *Press the finished seam edge over the metal template.*

2 *Put on the clamp and press again.*

3 *Set the crease and remove the template.*

Sewing Unlined Pockets

Finish the hem-facing edge of an unlined pocket by binding, serging, zigzagging, or turning the edge under ¼ in. and edgestitching. Let the fabric's weight help you determine the method; reserve edgestitching for lightweight fabrics such as linens.

Turn the hem to the right side along the upper foldline and stitch each end. Clip the upper fold of each seam allowance and press this small seam open with the point presser. Grade and turn the seam using a point turner to push the corners sharp.

Top-press on the cheese block to flatten the seamed edges and the upper hem fold. Machine topstitch along the lower edge of upper hem to hold it in place.

For square lower edges, press the remaining seam allowances under at ⅝ in. Press the bottom seam allowance up first so the side seam allowances will fold over the finished lower edge and so that no raw edges peek out from beneath the finished edges. For curved edges, see the sidebar.

Trim seams to ⅜ in. with the pinking shears or serge the seam edges. Grade seam allowances in the lower corners as necessary.

Sewing Pockets to the Jacket

Rather than hand-baste pockets in place, I prefer to use double-sided tape to hold them while I stitch. Make sure the package says you can stitch through the tape and that it will dissolve when dry cleaned. Apply double-sided tape to the outer edge on the wrong side of the pocket, using short pieces to go around the curve (**1**).

Remove the tape's paper backing and carefully place the pocket on the jacket markings. Use pins to mark the upper placement points. Measure to be sure that the pockets are in the same location on both sides of the jacket.

Lengthen the machine stitch and sew the pocket in place (**2**). Reinforce the upper pocket edges with a stitched rectangle. Begin stitching about 1 in. from the upper pocket edge. Sew across and into the pocket for about ¼ in.; pivot and stitch to the upper edge; pivot and stitch across ¼ in.; then pivot and stitch along the outside of the pocket.

Work carefully, and if necessary, slightly shorten the stitch length around curved corners. (Don't forget to lengthen it again for the straight areas.) Reverse the procedure when you reach the upper left side of the pocket.

If backstitching will be too obvious, pull the tail ends of the threads through and knot them on the wrong side. If the stitching hides well in the fabric, then backstitch.

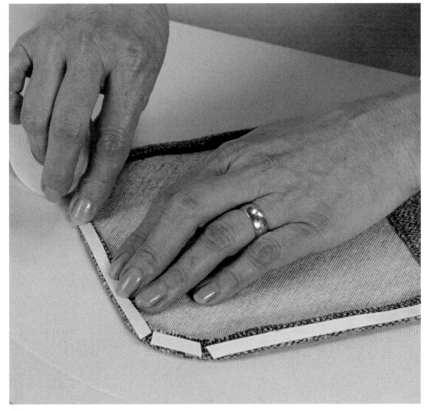

1 *Apply double-sided tape around the pocket edge.*

2 *Position the pocket and stitch from the right side. Stitch a small rectangle at the upper pocket edge to reinforce the opening*

The First Fitting

Fabric drapes and molds to the body differently from tissue, and now is the time to find any problems in the fit of the jacket. Before permanently stitching and pressing the side seams, go through this list carefully and make the necessary adjustments.

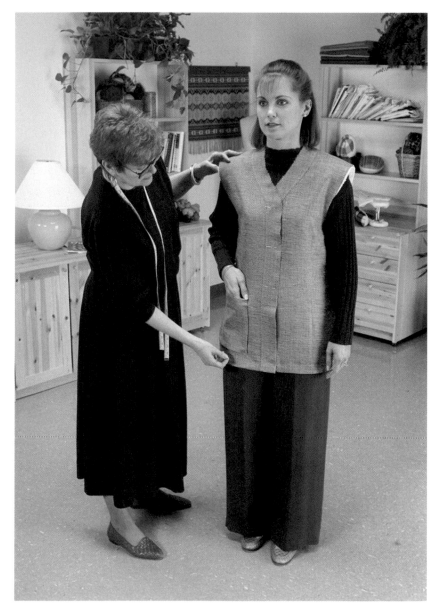

Preparing to Fit

Sleeves and facings are not sewn to the jacket for this fitting, but pin the hem in place to check the jacket length. Staystitch and clip the neck edge, if necessary, so it will lie flat.

As in pin-fitting with the tissue pattern pieces, try to fit the jacket over a blouse or sweater that you may actually wear underneath it. Pin the appropriate shoulder pads into the jacket, then place it on your body, matching and pinning together center-front lines at buttonhole placement marks.

Working from the top of the body down, carefully check all areas that were altered. Remember the list of alterations that was suggested in Chapter 3, pages 30-33? Get it out now to refresh your memory. Compare all your adjustments and evaluate their effectiveness. Be especially aware of width alterations to ensure that the jacket has the proper wearing and design ease, and check all lengths.

FITTING CHECKLIST

Place the shoulder line directly on top of the shoulder, extending at least ⅞ in. past the shoulder joint.

When you check the back shoulder width, it should be possible to pinch a ½-in. tuck in the fabric on either side of the shoulder blades **(1)**.

Check the bust for adequate ease; any darts or princess lines should point to or cross the bust point.

Check waist and hips for adequate ease **(2)**.

Make sure that the vertical seams hang at right angles to the floor and do not twist in any direction **(3)**.

Make sure that the jacket length is appropriate for your figure.

Slip your hand into the pocket to see that the placement is comfortable and natural **(4)**.

The chest-and-neck area should fit the body without gaping. (Remember that during construction, the neckline will be further tightened with an interfacing stay.)

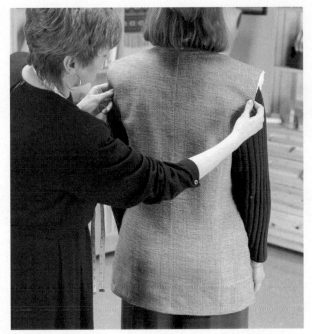

1 *Check the ease in the upper back.*

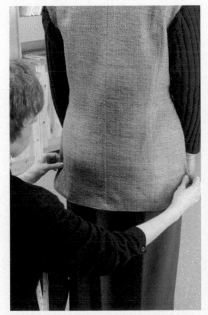

2 *Check the ease in the waist and hips.*

3 *Make sure that vertical seams hang straight.*

4 *Check the pocket and buttonhole placement*

Sewing Facings

With expert jacket facings, the neckline and chest lie over the front of the body without gaping, lower corners are flat, the seamline rolls slightly toward the facing, and front edges are as sharp and crisp as the fabric can stand.

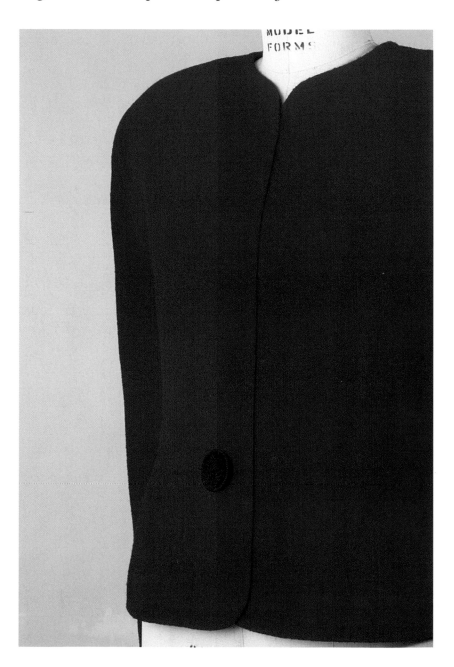

Sew the shoulder seams of the front and back facings. Press them open, then grade seam allowances to ³⁄₈ in.

The lower 2¹⁄₂ in. of the inner facing edge remains exposed, even after the jacket is hemmed and lined. In fabrics that don't easily ravel, you can leave it unfinished. If you fused interfacing using the finished-edge method, the lower edge is already finished; if you opted for the flat method, either serge, zigzag, or bind the lower 3 in. to 4 in. of the facing unit **(1)**.

With right sides together, pin the facing unit to the jacket, placing pins on the jacket side. On curved bottoms, avoid a "pulled" look at the bottom front edge by allowing for the jacket turn of the cloth (see page 61). Move the lower inner edge of the facing ¹⁄₈ in. to ¹⁄₄ in. from the jacket bottom edge before pinning the bottom of the facing to the jacket **(2)**. On squared-off bottoms, sew the vertical seam first and then the horizontal seam (see page 62).

Using the rotary cutter, on the lengthwise or most stable grain (*not* the bias), cut a ¹⁄₂-in. wide strip of fusible interfacing, tricot or nonwoven. For the length, measure from the top button or the waist on the jacket around the back of the neck to the opposite buttonhole. This strip is a stay tape for drawing up extra ease at the chest and/or waist, keeping the front from gaping as you wear the jacket and stabilizing the neck. (The cardigan-style jacket needs the chest drawn in so the neck hugs the body; the Chanel style needs the waist drawn in so the waist is closer to the body.)

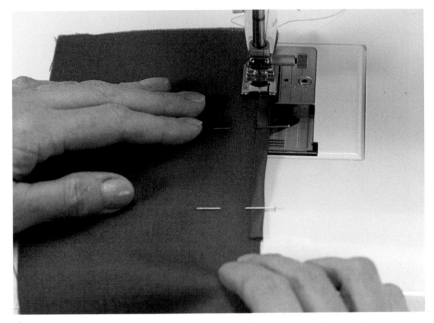

1 *Bind the bottom 4 in. of the facing if you haven't already used the finished-edge method.*

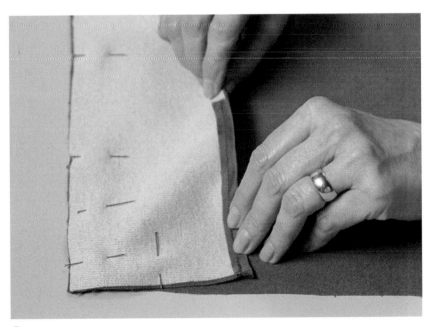

2 *Match the jacket and facing lower edges, then slide the facing edge up ¹⁄₈ in. to ¹⁄₄ in., and pin.*

3 *Stretch the stay tape as you sew.*

4 *Press the front-edge seam on the point presser.*

With the jacket side up, begin stitching at the lower edge, using a ⅝-in. seam allowance. Insert the stay: Center the interfacing strip over the seamline, resin side down. As you sew, gently pull the strip, stretching it slightly at the waist and/or chest (avoid stretching it on curved necklines, however). About 1 in. from the shoulder seam, relax the tape and sew, without pulling, across the back neck, 1 in. past the other shoulder seam. Again stretching the strip, sew to the buttonhole (3). Cut off the remaining strip and finish stitching to the lower edge of the facing.

Fuse the interfacing strip to the jacket, then press open the seam. Set the stitching around the entire facing and jacket edge at the same time.

Press the entire front-edge seam open on the point presser (4). Flatten the fabric further with the clapper, if needed.

Grade the remaining seam allowances after pressing. With pinking shears, notch out excess fabric from the outside curve of the lower edge. Clip the seam allowance in the inside curve of the neck.

Turn the jacket right-side out. The jacket front should roll under toward the facing. Use the steam iron and cheese block to top press and flatten the edge, first from the facing side, then from the jacket side. The clapper flattens these edges nicely (5).

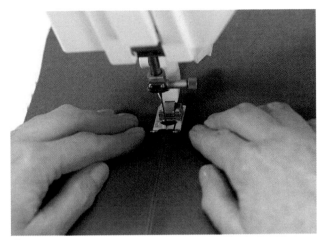

5 *Hold the facing edge as you press to ensure the turn-of-the-cloth.*

6 *Understitch the entire front facing, or just part of it.*

Understitching the facing is optional, but it further flattens the seam allowances and keeps them in place. It is easiest after all under-pressing and top-pressing are complete. Understitch the entire front edge or just from the button around to the buttonhole (**6**). If you plan to topstitch or edgestitch, understitching is unnecessary.

After the jacket is hemmed, topstitch or edgestitch. Secure the bottom 2½ in. of the facing edge with a small catchstitch. In unlined and partially lined jackets, pin the facing down in the bust and chest, turn the inner edge back ½ in., and loosely catchstitch. Do not sew over the facing edge or a ridge may form on the right side. For lined jackets, tack the facings down in the bust and chest, 1½ in. from the edge, to leave room for the lining to be sewn in. The lower edge will be secured after the lining is installed.

FACING CORNERS AND CURVES

Curved Edges
Shorten the stitch length and slow the machine speed to stitch smoothly around corners without having to stop and pivot. Cut a template of the corner from lightweight cardboard and use this as a guide for your stitching.

Square Corners
Your pattern may suggest one long L-shaped seam for this edge, but you can sew a better corner if you use two separate straight seams instead. See Sewing Square Corners on page 62 for details.

Use a cardboard template to sew a perfect curve.

Hemming the Jacket

A well-finished hem should be properly interfaced; it should lie flat and smooth with no telltale ridges or stitches; it should be well-pressed with no shine or matted look; its lower edge should be sharp.

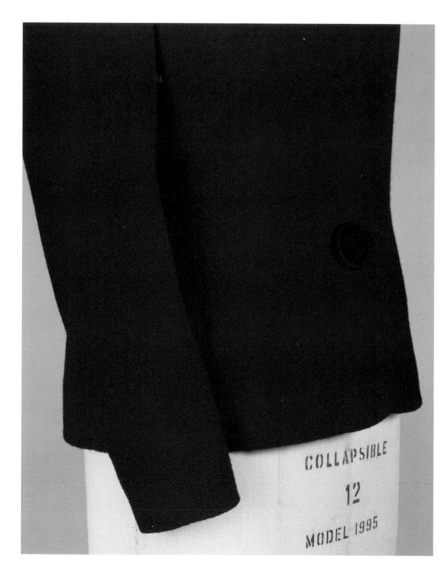

With the seam gauge, carefully measure and pin the hem depth, placing pins parallel and close to the upper edge of the hem. For smoothness, slightly shorten hem depth (about $1/8$ in) at seam intersections to allow for the turn of the cloth.

Set the hem fold on either the cheese block (for a very sharp crease) or a padded surface (for a softer look). Top-press the hem from inside the jacket, covering it with a press cloth just up to the pins (1). Avoid pressing over the pins or the upper hem edge, since this will leave impressions on the right side.

Reduce seam-allowance bulk in the hem by clipping into the hem fold and grading the hem-facing seam allowances to half the width of the original seams.

Serge, zigzag, or bind the hem-allowance edge if your jacket is to be partially lined or unlined. If your jacket is lined and the fabric is especially firm, the upper edge of the hem allowance may leave a ridge on the right side. Pink this edge to soften it.

Hem on the sewing machine or by hand. When the hem edge is left exposed, as in unlined jackets, machine-stitch the upper edge in place for durability (2). Stitch as close to the upper edge as possible (⅛ in. to ¼ in.), so the fabric won't crease with wear. Follow the topstitching instructions on page 51 and stitch from the wrong side (if your machine stitching is identical on both sides) to make sure you catch the hem's top edge.

If machine stitching is unsuitable, hand-stitch the hem using a traditional tailor's hem. For an unlined jacket, fold back the upper edge ¼ in. and catchstitch between the hem and the jacket. Use beeswaxed thread for strength, and make loose stitches, spaced at least ½ in. apart. Secure the hem to the machine stitching on the hem facing's upper edge.

Hand-sew a hem for a lined jacket the same way, with one difference: Turn the hem allowance back to half its depth, and catchstitch there (3). Leave ¾ to 1 in. of fabric at the hem facing's upper edge to make easy work of inserting the lining.

In partially lined or unlined jackets, secure the bottom edges of the front facings to the hem allowance. In lined jackets, secure these edges after the lining is in, as described on page 105.

1 *Press the pinned hem with a press cloth, taking care not to go over the pins.*

2 *Topstitch the jacket along the upper edge of the hem allowance.*

3 *To hand-sew the hem, catchstitch between the hem and the jacket body.*

Sewing the Sleeves

A well-set jacket sleeve has a smooth, high crown and is free of wrinkles, puckers, and folds around the upper arm.

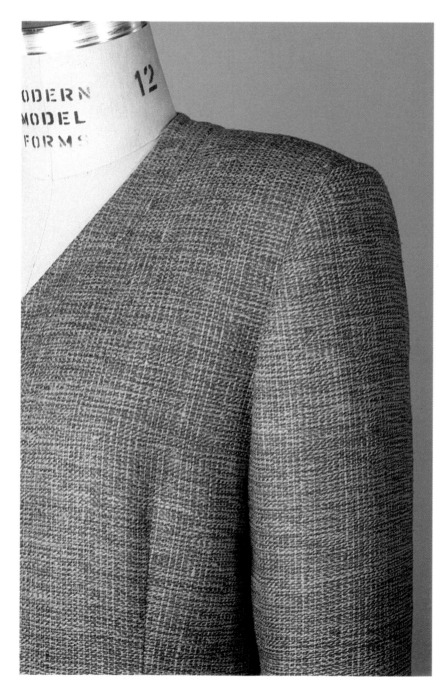

Preparing the Sleeves

If your sleeve doesn't have a vent, you need only stitch the underarm seam and hem the sleeve.

Press the hem allowance up before sewing any seams. This is easiest when the sleeve is still flat (**1**).

Open the hem, and sew and press the sleeve underarm seams, beginning with the vent seam if there is one. Reduce bulk by grading the seams in the hem allowance to half their width (**2**).

After top-pressing the seams, with the sleeve still over a seam roll right-side out, fold the hem under along the previously creased fold. Re-press this fold at each seam to sharpen the creases.

Hem the sleeves by machine- or hand-stitching as on pages 49-51.

1 *It's far easier to press the sleeve hem when the sleeve is still flat, before it is sewn.*

A READY-TO-WEAR SLEEVE VENT

Thanks to garment industry designers, the traditional mitered sleeve vent has given way to a new vent that is easier and faster to sew. Although it doesn't open completely, as does a traditional vent, this vent presses flat because there is little bulk, it has no corners to miter, and it allows the lining to be machine-stitched at the wrist opening. Best of all, it still looks like a vent.

This vent can be added to all two-piece sleeves, one-piece sleeves with the underarm seam offset to the outer edge, and to raglan and kimono sleeves with an overarm seam. To simulate the look of a traditional vent, the finished vent opening should be at least 3 in. long (beginning at the hem fold) and $1\frac{3}{8}$ in. wide. Instructions for adding this vent to a sleeve are detailed on the following pages.

2 *Trim and grade seams in the sleeve hem allowance.*

A READY-TO-WEAR SLEEVE VENT (cont'd.)

Revising a Traditional Vent

If your pattern has a sleeve vent extending into the hem, turn up the hem allowance on the hem foldline, and trace the vent fold and placement lines on the hem allowance. Unfold the hem and draw a ⅝-in. seam allowance beyond this tracing. Trim away excess pattern tissue.

Inserting a New Vent

If your pattern has no vent, it's easy to add one. Mark the finished vent length plus ⅝-in. seam allowance on the sleeve stitching line and extend this area out to the finished width plus ⅝ in. for the seam. Curve the lower edges for stitching.

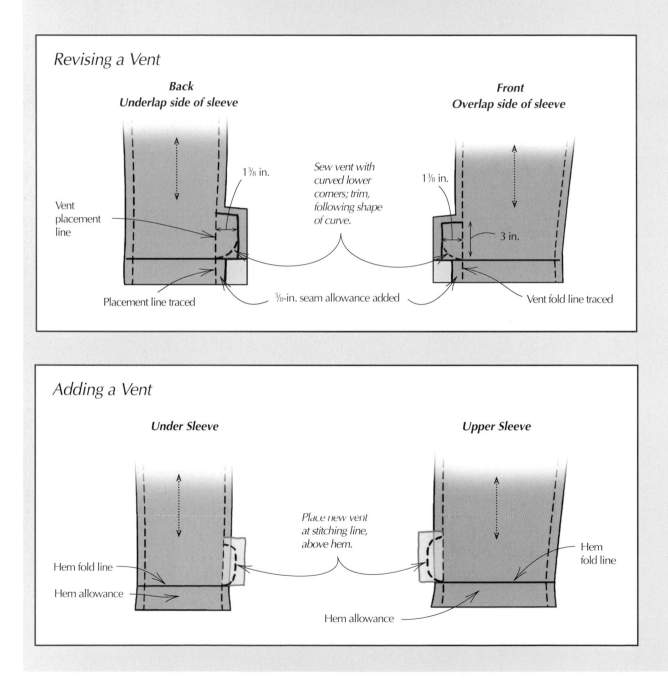

Revising a Vent

Back
Underlap side of sleeve

Front
Overlap side of sleeve

1⅜ in.

Sew vent with curved lower corners; trim, following shape of curve.

1⅜ in.

3 in.

Vent placement line

Placement line traced

⅝-in. seam allowance added

Vent fold line traced

Adding a Vent

Under Sleeve

Upper Sleeve

Place new vent at stitching line, above hem.

Hem fold line

Hem fold line

Hem allowance

Hem allowance

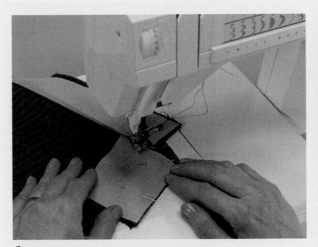

1 *Stitch the interfaced vent seam first.*

2 *Clip back seam allowance.*

Sewing the Vent

Fuse interfacing to the hem and both sides of the sleeve vent to fold and placement lines. Press the hem allowance in place.

Mark stitching lines along the vent, curving the stitching at the lower vent corner over to the hem fold. This curve minimizes fabric bulk at the hem fold, especially after trimming and grading.

Open the hem allowance; sew along seam and vent stitching lines while the seam is flat **(1).** Diagonally clip the upper back seam allowance to the corner of the stitching line **(2).** Press open the sleeve seam above the vent; press seams in the hem to one side and grade. For bulky fabric, clip the back seam allowance in the hem to the corner, and press open. Apply Fray-Check adhesive if necessary. Grade the back seam allowance around the vent.

Turn the sleeve right-side out. Carefully crease on the vent foldline and press the vent toward the sleeve front, making sure fold line meets placement line on sleeve back **(3).** Place over the seam roll and top-press the seam at the same time. Turn the hem allowance up; re-press the fold at the vent's lower edge **(4).** Use the cheese block and clapper to sharpen the crease.

Open the hem out flat and stitch the remaining seam of a two-piece sleeve. Press and grade seam allowances in the hem area. Fold the hem up and carefully re-press the fold along the seam section. Finish the sleeves as explained on pages 82-87.

3 *Steam-press vent using a press cloth.*

4 *After turning up hem allowance, re-press vent fold.*

Sewing Set-in Sleeves

A set-in sleeve needs extra ease in the sleeve cap, for movement in the upper arm and proper draping of the sleeve fabric. A symmetrical, uniformly rounded cap is easier than ever to achieve, because a bias canvas strip absorbs the ease for you.

Preparing the Cap Trim any fabric that extends beyond the sleeve-cap edge **(1)**. This will give you a smooth outer curve to follow.

Cut a bias strip of nonfusible hair canvas, $1\frac{1}{2}$ in. wide and long enough to reach around the sleeve cap from notch to notch. Soften the hair canvas by soaking it in a basin of water (follow the directions for preshrinking fabrics on page 17), or dampen with the iron's spray and press dry. For directions on cutting bias strips, see page 55.

On the wrong side of the fabric, position the bias strip $\frac{1}{8}$ in. from the sleeve's cut edge, starting at one of the notches. Using a $\frac{1}{2}$-in. seam allowance (measured from the sleeve's cut edge) and a basting stitch, anchor the strip at the notch with a few machine stitches. Machine-baste, stretching the strip firmly and evenly, so there will be

If the hair canvas is too heavy for your fabric or shows through to the outside, substitute a bias strip of self-fabric, nylon tricot, or lamb's wool.

1 *Trim any fabric that extends beyond the sleeve cap edge.*

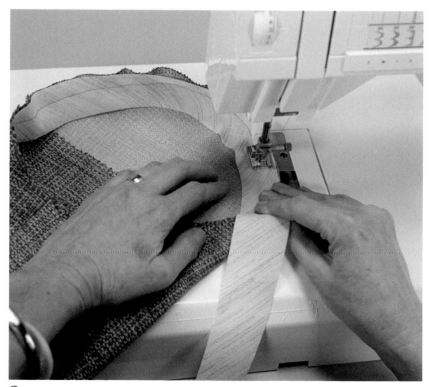

2 *Stretch the bias strip as you machine-baste it in.*

1 in. to 2 in. to trim away at the end **(2)**. The top 1 in. of the sleeve cap should not be eased, so don't stretch the strip for $^1/_2$ in. on either side of the cap center. End and anchor the basting at the second notch.

Trim the excess bias strip at the notch (1 in. to 2 in.). When the bias strip relaxes, the sleeve eases evenly. To check the easing, place your hand inside the sleeve, positioning the cap over your fingers. Horizontal and vertical yarns should be at right angles; the sleeve cap should be dimple-free; and the stitching line should be flat **(3)**.

To shrink out excess fullness in the seam allowance, place the cap over the ham or cheese block and dampen only the seam allowance with the dauber or steam iron. With a dry iron, shrink out the fullness and flatten the seam allowance by pressing with a raising and lowering motion **(4)**. Don't press beyond the stitching line into the crown of the sleeve, and allow the sleeve to dry completely before laying it out flat. The strip remains in the sleeve cap to maintain the shape and prevent the seam edge from forming a ridge on the right side of the sleeve.

Stretch the bias strip with the left hand and use the right hand to guide the sleeve cap beneath the presser foot. After stitching, the bias strip relaxes and draws up the sleeve ease.

3 *Check the shape of the sleeve cap to make sure the ease is even where it should be.*

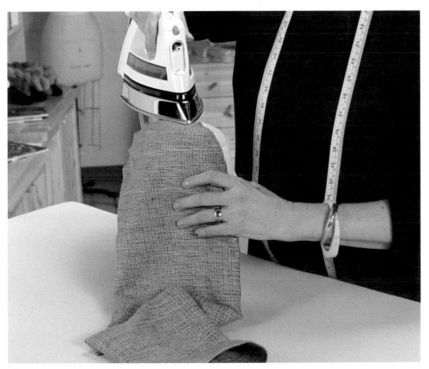

4 *Shrink out excess fullness in the sleeve cap by pressing with a dry iron.*

EASING A SLEEVE CAP THE TRADITIONAL WAY

The traditional method for easing a sleeve cap is to sew in two parallel rows of stitches, then pull them gently into the correct configuration. Since the sleeve lining doesn't need a bias strip in its crown, it can be traditionally eased as outlined here. If you find working on the fashion fabric sleeve with the bias canvas strip difficult, you may want to use this gathering method instead.

Place the sleeve cap under the presser foot with the wrong side down. Machine-baste two rows between notches. Place the first row just inside the stitching line, the second row ⅛ in. from the first row, in the allowance **(1)**. Leave 3-in. tails of threads hanging from each end.

Working from inside the sleeve cap (the bobbin thread is on this side and its thread draws easier than the needle's), grasp two thread tails and draw the sleeve fabric up as if you were gathering it. Ease to within ½ in. of the sleeve-cap center **(2)**. Repeat at the other thread ends.

Working from the sleeve-cap center to each notch, ease the excess fabric from the stitching line to the seam allowance with your fingers **(3)**.

When the seamline is fairly smooth, measure the distance between notches on the jacket armhole and compare it to the distance between notches on the sleeve cap. Continue adjusting ease until the cap measurement matches the armhole measurement.

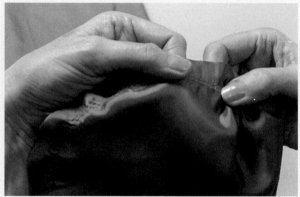

2 *Gather the fabric along lines of stitching to ease the excess fabric in the sleeve cap.*

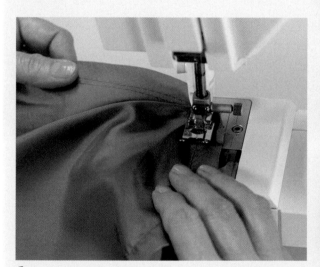

1 *Sew two rows of gathering stitches in the cap.*

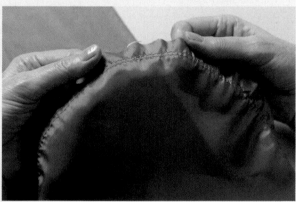

3 *This is how a properly eased sleeve lining should look.*

Setting the Sleeve Once you've eased the cap with a bias strip, you can set the sleeve into the jacket without any tedious hand-basting. Use the pinning method below so you can check the ease before you sew.

With right sides together, match the sleeve underarm to the jacket and pin between notches on the sleeve. Place the pins ⅝ in. from the outer edge and parallel to the seamline (**1**).

Reach inside the jacket and grasp the top of the sleeve and the shoulder seam. Turn the jacket to the wrong side and, working from inside the sleeve, match and pin the sleeve-cap center to the shoulder seam (**2**). Pin the upper sleeve cap between the notches on each side, placing pins parallel (**3**).

1 *Place pins between the notches, parallel to the seamline.*

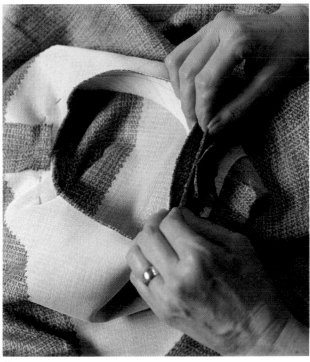

2 *Working from inside the sleeve, pin sleeve cap to armhole between notches.*

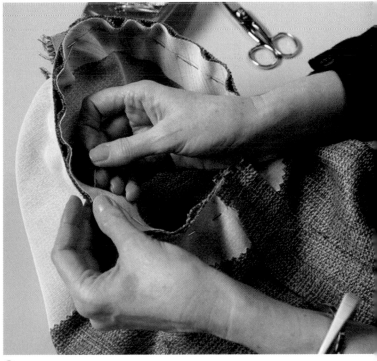

3 *Sleeve is fully pinned into jacket.*

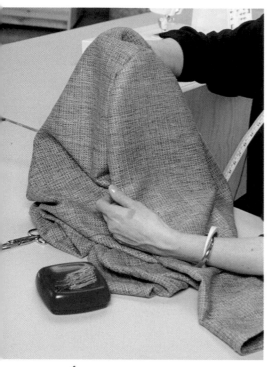

4 *Check the grainline of the sleeve and jacket together, to be sure that the yarns run horizontally across the back and around the sleeve.*

Turn the jacket right-side out. Check that grainline is horizontal across the sleeve and back of jacket, and inspect the sleeve crown for dimples (**4**). Put on the jacket and check the sleeve. (In high-cut underarms, replace pins with hand-basting so you don't stick yourself.)

From inside the sleeve, machine-stitch, beginning at one notch, following the underarm to the second notch, and around the sleeve cap. Without breaking the stitching, stitch a ¹/₂-in. seam allowance between the notches for reinforcement. Set the stitch, allowing the iron only ¹/₈ in. into the sleeve cap.

Between notches, trim the underarm seam to ¹/₄ in. to ³/₈ in. If your fabric ravels, zigzag ¹/₄ in. to ³/₈ in. from the seamline before trimming it (**5**).

Place the jacket underarm right-side up on the ham and fold the sleeve back so allowances face the sleeve. Cover with a press cloth, moisten, and top-press the underarm seamline between notches (**6**).

Place the upper part of the sleeve cap over the ham, right-side out, with the seam allowance falling toward the sleeve cap. Hold the iron over (not *on*) the well of the seam to force steam into the fabric (**7**). Finger-press the seamline, making a soft roll in the sleeve cap (**8**). Leave the sleeve on the ham until the fabric is dry and the roll is set. The hair canvas used to ease the sleeve cap may provide enough rounding support to the upper-cap roll. If the sleeve droops or pulls on the jacket shoulder, insert a sleeve header made of needlepunch apparel batting or lamb's wool (see page 89).

5 *Trim the underarm seam between notches. Note the zigzag reinforcement.*

6 *Top-press the underarm seam.*

EASING SOLUTIONS

When you hold the eased cap over your fingers, the horizontal and vertical yarns should be at right angles. If horizontal yarns pull toward the sleeve top (the usual problem), clip a stitch or two of the basting threads where the yarns are distorted. Then examine the sleeve-cap seam allowance. The outer edge should be rippled, since the bias strip forced the ease into the seam allowance and kept the stitching line flat. This is crucial for a nicely rounded crown.

If there is too much tension in the stitching, the cap will be too small for the armhole (see photo at right).

If the bias strip did not completely ease the sleeve cap, there will be some extra ease between the sleeve center and the notches. This ease can be taken up when pinning if it's no more than $1/2$ in. on each side. If, however, there is more ease than this, the bias strip wasn't stretched hard enough when first stitched to the cap, and you won't be able to stitch the sleeve smoothly into the armhole. Remove the sleeve and rip the basting from the bias strip. Ease the sleeve cap to the bias again, pulling more firmly this time.

If there is too much tension in the ease, the yarns will curve upward.

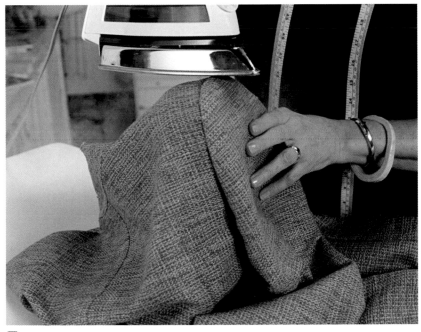

7 *Hold the iron above the armhole seamline to steam-shape the cap.*

8 *Finger-press the seamline to form a soft roll in the cap.*

SLEEVE HEADERS

Sleeve headers are strips of thick fabric or batting that lift and support the sleeve cap and enhance the sleeve's drape. This ready-to-wear technique is easy to do and eliminates the bulky seam allowances of traditional straight-cut heads.

Use your jacket sleeve pattern to draft the sleeve-cap shape from notch to notch, as the diagram shows. Cut two 1½-in. wide strips of needlepunch apparel batting or lamb's wool in this shape and length.

Center the header inside the sleeve cap with one long edge matched to the cap edge. Permanently baste it to the cap-seam allowance, close to the machine stitching. Make your stitches at least ¼ in. long, and keep them loose. When you push the seam allowance into the sleeve, the head gently folds into two layers to support the cap.

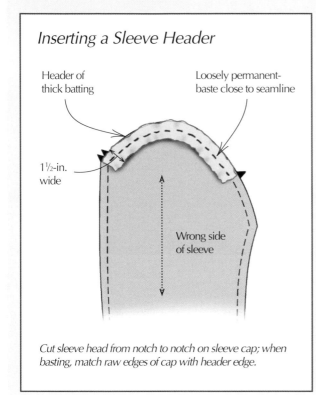

Inserting a Sleeve Header

Header of thick batting

Loosely permanent-baste close to seamline

1½-in. wide

Wrong side of sleeve

Cut sleeve head from notch to notch on sleeve cap; when basting, match raw edges of cap with header edge.

Cut a sleeve header in the shape of your sleeve cap.

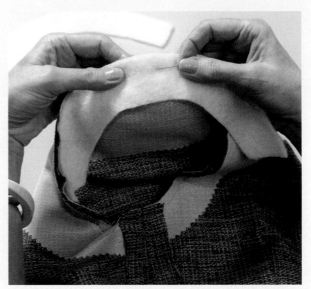

Pin the header into the sleeve cap before basting.

Shoulder Pads

Together, sleeve headers and shoulder pads stabilize and contour the shoulders and sleeve caps. Inserting shoulder pads often has an immediate and dramatic impact on a jacket's fit; what seemed overly loose and droopy can become fitted and smart in just minutes. Always use shoulder pads if your pattern envelope lists them as a notion, because the jacket has been designed for them.

Padding Set-in Sleeves Try on the jacket and place the shoulder-pad center beneath the shoulder seam, extending it $5/8$ in. into the sleeve cap. The straight edge goes toward the armhole, and the widest part faces the jacket front, stabilizing the chest area. Pin along the shoulder line on the outside of the jacket. Remove the jacket and examine the pad position. Adjust as necessary and anchor well with pins.

Shoulder pads of ready-to-wear jackets are usually machine-stitched in place, giving excellent support to the sleeve-cap roll and holding the seam allowance where it belongs, in the sleeve. This requires more skill, and I don't suggest it (at least not initially). If you have trouble keeping the seam allowance in the sleeve cap, loosely stab-stitch the entire outer edge of the shoulder pad to the seam allowance, just inside the armhole stitching.

At the pad center and ends, loosely stab-stitch the pad to the seam allowance, just inside the stitching line. Catchstitch the curved edge to the shoulder seam allowance. Lay the neck facing over the pad, then fold it back to half its width, catchstitching the pad and facing together. Leave at least 1 in. of the facing edge unattached for installing the lining.

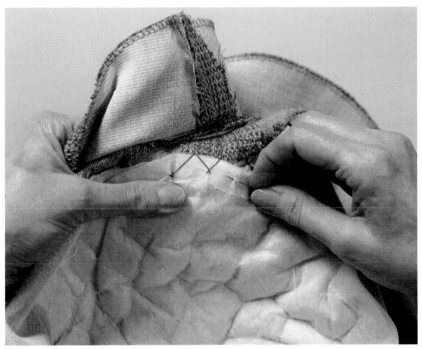

Catchstitch shoulder pads to secure them to shoulder seams.

Sewing Kimono, Raglan, and Dropped-Shoulder Sleeves

Kimono, raglan sleeves, and dropped-shoulder sleeves are easier to sew than set-in sleeves, because the sleeve cut is completely different. In kimono sleeves, the entire sleeve is cut as part of the jacket body; in the raglan style, the sleeve is attached to the upper jacket body. The dropped-shoulder sleeve has a short sleeve cap and an armhole that encircles the arm, and the seam allowance extends at least 1½ in. from the body and "drops" off the shoulder.

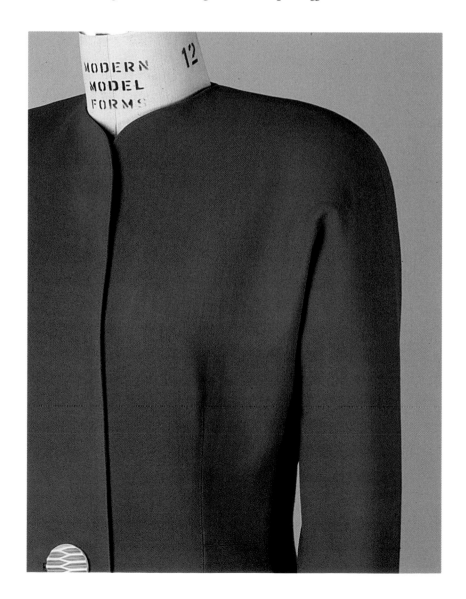

Kimono and Raglan Sleeves

Kimono and raglan sleeves differ primarily in the underarms. The raglan style retains the underarm of a set-in sleeve, resulting in a smoother underarm and silhouette. Kimono sleeves may range from tailored and sleek to loose-fitting and fluid, depending upon the underarm curve and shoulder slope.

The two styles have one thing in common: The sleeve underarm and jacket side seam are often sewn in one continuous seam. Because they have no true sleeve cap, they all crease at the underarm.

With only two straight seams, the kimono is undoubtedly the easiest sleeve to sew. The raglan and dropped-shoulder sleeves are set in while they are still flat, making their assembly fast and easy. However, raglan sleeves have a shaped underarm curve, making them a bit more difficult. The dropped-shoulder style approaches traditional set-in sleeves, but the sleeve cap requires little or no easing.

Reinforcing the Underarm Seam

Sew overarm seams; complete sleeve vents, if necessary. Edgestitch or topstitch seam now, while the sleeve is flat. Press the hem folds.

If your pattern suggests completely finishing the raglan or dropped-shoulder sleeve, and then setting it as you would a fitted sleeve, the underarm is probably cut fairly high, so sewing the underarm and side as one seam would distort the fit. In this case, follow the pattern guide.

Sew underarm seams from the jacket hem to the wrist. To reinforce the underarm seams of an unlined kimono-style jacket, restitch around the curve very close to the first stitching. Trim seams to $5/8$ in., since pressing curved 1-in. seams is difficult. Press seams open and then toward the back. Trim seam allowances to $3/8$ in. to $1/2$ in., then serge, zigzag, or bind. Try to avoid clipping the seams for they will not wear well.

For a lined jacket, center a narrow strip of interfacing over the stitching line, attaching the strip as the seam is sewn (1). Fuse strip in place, then clip and press seams open (2).

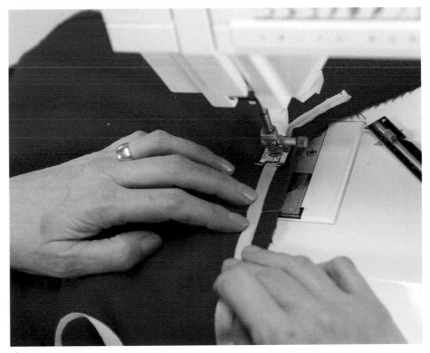

1 Staystitch a strip of fusible interfacing to the underarm seam of a kimono-style jacket for reinforcement.

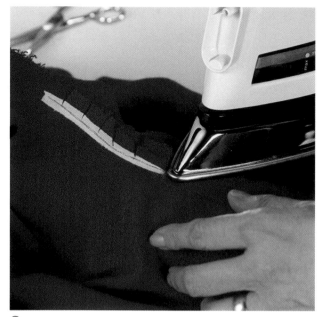

2 *Clip underarm seam, then press.*

3 *Reinforce the underarm seam by topstitching on both sides of the seamline. Make sure you catch the seam allowances in the stitching.*

Reinforce the underarm seam by topstitching along both sides of the seamline, forming a narrow rectangle **(3)**.

After stitching the raglan sleeve to the body of the jacket, clip at the underarm notches so the upper portion of the raglan seam can be pressed in one direction.

Hold seam allowances in place from the neck edge to the notches with edgestitching or topstitching.

If the underarm seam of a raglan-style jacket is joined from the wrist to the hem, reinforce and finish as for the unlined kimono sleeve.

Dropped-Shoulder Sleeves To prepare the jacket, join front to back at the shoulder, and edgestitch and topstitch if desired. If there is any sleeve-cap ease, use the traditional easing method (page 84). Press hem fold in place. Do not sew the sleeve underarm seam unless the pattern instructs you to.

With right sides together, place the sleeve cap in the jacket, matching the cap center to the shoulder seam and keeping underarm edges even. Stitch. Press seam allowances open, then to one side. Press cap allowances that are fairly smooth into the sleeve;

When pressing the underarm curves, use only the iron tip and a point presser to avoid pressing creases in the jacket body.

Pin on the sleeve for a dropped-shoulder jacket using the flat method.

edgestitch. Press fuller cap allowances toward the jacket body; edgestitch.

Join front to back by sewing the underarm seam from the jacket hem to the wrist. Reinforce 3 in. to 4 in. of the underarm curve by sewing again close to the first stitching. Clip the curve; press seam allowances open and then toward the back. Edgestitch or topstitch to hold seam allowances in place. Finish edges if jacket is to be unlined.

Padding Kimono, Raglan, or Dropped-Shoulder Sleeves

Try on the jacket, and position the shoulder pad over the ball of your shoulder. From the outside, pin in place along the overarm seam.

Turn the jacket to the wrong side and loosely catchstitch the shoulder pad to the overarm seam allowance from the neck to the end of the shoulder (**1**). Be careful not to stitch out in the curve of the pad, since the jacket should move freely in this area. On the other end, catchstitch the shoulder pad beneath the neck facings (**2**).

Covered Shoulder Pads for Raglan, Kimono, or Dropped-Shoulder Sleeves

These curved pads require a separate bias piece of fabric for each side. Place the fabric over the pad, pinning it loosely in place, and fold a small dart at the outer curve (**3**). Stitch the dart by hand or machine. Trim the outer edges ½ in. wider than the pad. Zigzag or serge around the outer edge of the shoulder pad (**4**).

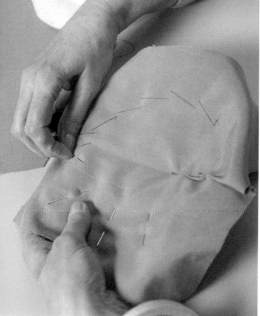

1 *Catchstitch shoulder pad to sleeve cap.*

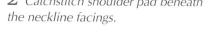

2 *Catchstitch shoulder pad beneath the neckline facings.*

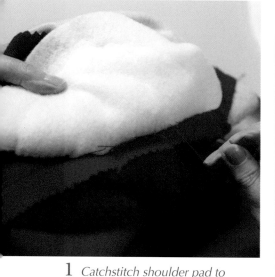

3 *Make a dart to shape the cover fabric of the shoulder pad. Baste fabric directly onto the shoulder pad.*

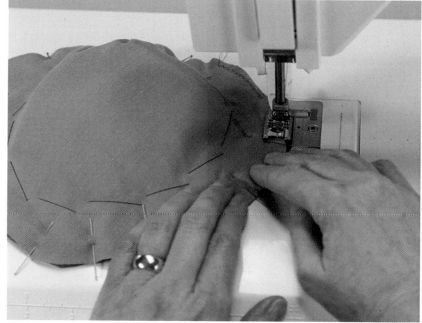

4 *Machine-stitch the cover over the pad using zigzag stitch.*

Bagging the Jacket Lining

Linings can be quickly and easily inserted into the jacket by "bagging." This garment-industry method for assembling and attaching a full lining by machine gets its name from the "bag" that forms as you pull and turn jacket sections through the jacket's hem and sleeve openings. The lining will fit into the jacket as if it had been carefully positioned and hand-sewn.

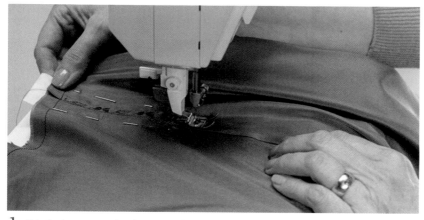

1 *Stitch the center-back seam, then, for a classic touch, add decorative machine stitching.*

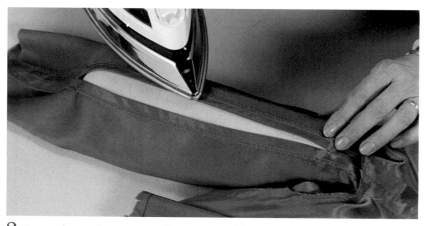

2 *Leave the underarm seam lining open; fold and press the seam allowances toward the wrong side.*

3 *Staystitch, then clip the curved necklines as much as necessary to make joining easy.*

Putting the Lining Together

Machine-sewn linings are more secure, more durable, and take far less time to insert than traditional linings. Use either a standard sewing machine or a serger to assemble the lining. Press seam allowances open or to one side, and press the lining darts in the direction opposite of jacket darts to minimize bulk.

Machine-stitch the center-back pleat, varying the stitch length between basting and regular stitching. Regular stitching can be used 1½ in. to 3 in. in the neck, waist, and hem with the remainder of the pleat basted closed. Set stitch and press pleat to left back.

If lining has a pleat that tapers to the waistline, stitch the outer seam allowance at ⅝ in., tapering from neck to waist. For a classic touch, add decorative machine stitching at upper 1½ in. to 3 in. of pleat and at the waist (support the back of the lining fabric with tear-away stabilizer if necessary) (**1**).

Stitch both sleeve underarm seams, but leave one open for 10 in. to 12 in., about 1½ in. below the armhole. Serge or zigzag the opening's raw edges to keep them from fraying as you work. Fold and press the opening's seam allowances toward the wrong side (**2**).

Ease the sleeve caps with machine stitching (see pages 82-86), sew the sleeves in the armholes, then press the seam allowances toward the sleeve cap. Reinforce and trim the lower armhole seam.

4 *Before you begin lining the jacket, make sure the shell is finished.*

Staystitch and clip the front and back lining along the necklines for easier joining to the jacket (3).

Use the following checklist to make sure the jacket shell is complete before you begin attaching the lining (4).

- pockets attached
- lower 3 in. of front facing finished

Sew all vertical seams ⅛ in. to ¼ in. narrower than the seam allowances dictate to allow more ease in the lining body.

- facings understitched
- inner edge of facing tacked at chest
- hems catchstitched in center of hem depth
- sleeve caps steamed and finger-pressed
- sleeve underarms trimmed between notches
- shoulder pads and sleeve headers inserted
- buttons sewn to sleeve vents
- final pressing done
- piping sewn to inner edge of facing

ADDING PIPING

Piping the inner edge of the facing is strictly decorative, but it is a distinctive finish that enhances your jacket's overall appearance.

The technique is easy. Use purchased piping if you can find a color you like, or make your own with lining fabric. To make piping, fold 1¾-in. wide bias strips of fabric around a soft, small-diameter yarn or cord. (See page 55 for directions on cutting bias strips.) Stitch close to the cord with a zipper or piping foot (**1**).

For the piping length, measure around the facing inner edge from hem to hem and add 2 in.

Pin the piping on the right side of the inner edge of front and back facings, matching raw edges. Leave 1 in. of piping extending below the jacket's bottom

edge on each side. Sew the piping to the facings on the ⅝-in. seamline. Begin and end at least ¾ in. below the raw edge of the hem allowance. Stitch as close to the cord as possible, using a zipper or piping foot (**2**).

When you sew the lining to the jacket, place the lining over the piping and match it to the front and back facings. You will have piping sandwiched between the lining and facing. Align the raw edges of the lining and jacket, bring the loose end of the piping over the lining, trim, then stitch the lining (see photo 2 on facing page).

1 *Stitch bias strips of fabric around yarn or cord to make piping.*

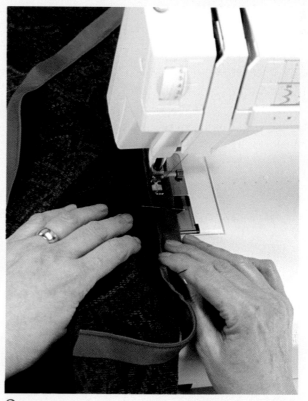

2 *Stitch the piping to the front and back facing edges.*

Attaching the Lining to the Facing

Turn the jacket body wrong-side out and place it flat, with front facings on top. With right sides together, match the lining to the front and back facings and pin it in place along the entire facing edge **(1)**.

At the lower front-facing edge, fold up the lining hem so that the raw edges of the lining hem and the jacket are even. If piping has been used, fold the loose end up and over the lining. Trim **(2)**.

Stitch the lining to the entire front edge with a ⅝-in. seam allowance. As you sew, keep the jacket bulk to the left of the needle. If you stitch

1 *Align the raw edges of the lining hem with those of the jacket. Pin the lining to the jacket facing, right sides together.*

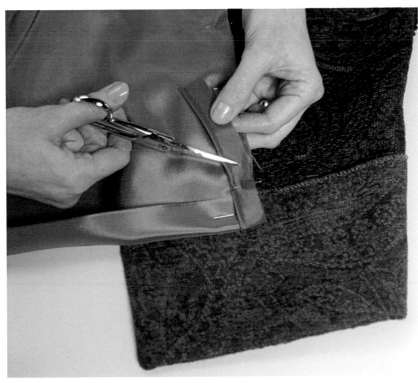

2 *Fold the piping up over the lining and trim.*

3 Use a ⅝-in. seam to sew the lining to the front edge.

4 Push the sleeve linings into the jacket sleeves.

with the lining side up, the sewing machine's feed dogs will help ease the jacket to the lining. But if you've piped your jacket, you'll want to stitch with the interfacing side up (3), so you can stitch exactly over the piping seamline.

Set the stitching with a warm iron (see page 57). Turn the jacket and lining right-side out and push the sleeve linings into the jacket sleeves (4).

From the right side, place a seam roll between the jacket and facing. Press the facing/lining seam smooth, with both seam allowances falling toward the side seams. This keeps the inner edge of the facing flat and smooth. If you used piping, press carefully to avoid flattening it.

If necessary, ease the jacket fabric to the lining between the hem and shoulder. The jacket fabric may have stretched with handling during construction.

Completing the Sleeves

To keep the lining from twisting in the sleeve as you work, pin the seams of the sleeve and lining together about 6 in. above the sleeve hem.

With the jacket right side out, turn up the raw edge of the sleeve lining ⅝ in., so right sides of jacket and lining are together as if for stitching. Hold them together with one hand (1).

With the other hand, reach between the lining and jacket fabrics, from the jacket hem up through the sleeve. Grasp the two hem allowances from your first hand, keeping their right sides together. Pull the entire sleeve unit back through the jacket bottom.

Keep right sides together. Ease and pin the jacket fabric to the lining, matching underarm seams and hem bottoms, working around the entire circumference (2). Machine-stitch using a ⅝-in. seam, with the jacket fabric facing down.

Set the stitching. Push the sleeve back through the bottom and turn it right-side out. A jump hem (or ease tuck) forms at the lower edge of the sleeve lining to allow ease when wearing the jacket. This tuck can be lightly pressed or allowed to find its own crease when the jacket is worn.

1 *Turn up raw edges of sleeve and lining hems, and hold them with one hand.*

2 *Pin the lining and sleeve hems together and stitch.*

Completing the Bottom Edge

The jacket and lining hems are stitched together in sections. With right sides facing, match and pin the jacket and lining hems together, from each side seam to the front facings (1). Using a ⅝-in.

seam, stitch to within 1½ in. of front facing seam (2). This small opening keeps the lining from pulling up in this corner. Set the stitch and turn right-side out.

The jacket back, between side seams, remains to be sewn. Reach into the opening in the sleeve lining and pull these back hems

1 Pin the jacket and lining hems together from side seam to front facing.

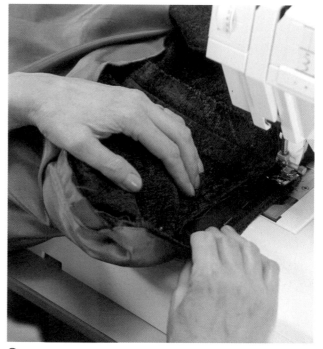

2 Stitch jacket front hem to lining, using a ⅝-in. seam.

through, keeping right sides together **(3)**. (This is the "bag" in "bagging the lining.") Pin, then stitch, using a ⅝-in. seam **(4)**. Ease if necessary. Set the stitch.

Push the hem back through the sleeve opening so the jacket is right-side out. The lining will form a jump pleat across the entire lower edge. Lightly press the jump pleat into place **(5)**.

The lining should not be tight. If you have excess ease across the lower jacket hem, you may need to let out the lining seams slightly. This will prevent the lining from pulling the outer fabric when the two are sewn together.

3 *Pull the back jacket and lining hems through the sleeve-lining opening.*

4 *Pin together the hems pulled through the sleeve lining.*

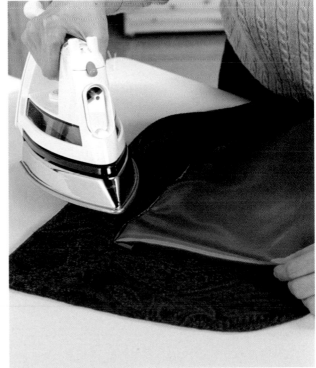

5 *Lightly press jump pleat formed by lining and jacket hems.*

Finishing the Jacket

If you forgot to fold and press the underarm lining seam allowances to the wrong side of the sleeve opening, do it now.

Close and pin the open lining seam: Bring folded edges together, keeping seam allowances flat and turned inside. Edgestitch through all layers close to the fold (1). The tiny ridge that this produces will be invisible on the right side.

Where the underarm meets the side seam, match the lining and the jacket. From the jacket's right side, pin through all thicknesses, making sure side and armhole seams are aligned (2). Note that the extra underarm ease allows the lining to fit up and over the jacket underarm seam without pulling the outer fabric of the jacket or the sleeve. To keep the lining in place, stitch in the ditch about 1/2 in. below the armhole and along the jacket side seam.

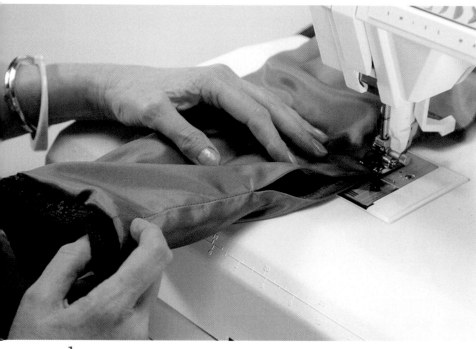

1 *Close the sleeve lining opening by edgestitching through all layers.*

2 *Match underarm lining and jacket seams, then pin to stitch in the ditch to hold lining in place.*

Insert a small square of fusible web under the front facing below the lining hem (3). This small segment of facing is the only place on a lined jacket where a raw edge is visible. In ready-to-wear jackets, this raw edge is often turned under ¼ in. and fused, but in most fabrics, this turned edge produces a ridge. I prefer to leave the facing edge flat, then catchstitch it in place as in custom-tailored jackets.

Don't forget to remove basting from the center-back pleat. The regular stitching will hold the pleat together at the neck, waist, and hem.

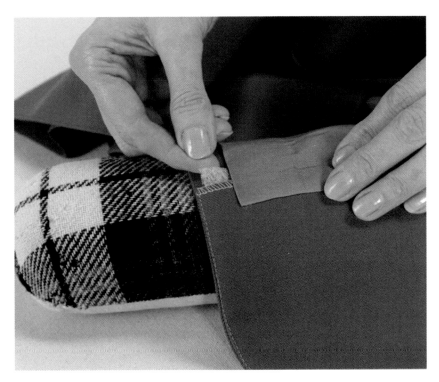

3 *Secure the small section of the facing that is visible with a square of fusible interfacing, then catchstitch.*

ALTERNATIVE LININGS

A fully lined jacket is the ultimate in luxury but requires extra time to make. Faster options include leaving the jacket unlined, lining only the sleeves, or partially lining the chest and back. Don't be afraid to revise the pattern to suit your needs better, especially if you are sewing a casual, unstructured jacket or are pressed for time. Instructions on pages 34-38 detail how to revise the pattern pieces.

No Lining
Follow the construction sequence for an unlined jacket (page 48), and use covered shoulder pads. Consider the finished-edge method for fusing interfacings to the facings. For a distinctive look, use special seams or finishes (experiment with several before sewing to see what you like most). Try to finish all seams and hem edges in a like manner.

Sleeves-Only Lining
Complete as for an unlined jacket, but cut a lining for the sleeves (page 37). Don't insert shoulder pads yet. Sew the lining underarm seam. Ease the lining sleeve cap with threads (page 84). Press the sleeve cap seam allowance under to the wrong side.

Turn the jacket and sleeve lining wrong-side out. Match and pin the sleeve lining to the upper edge of the jacket sleeve hem, right sides together. Machine stitch and press. Turn the jacket right-side out; pull the sleeve lining up to meet the jacket sleeve cap.

ALTERNATIVE LININGS (*cont'd.*)

Match the lining to the jacket shoulder and underarm seams. Pin the sleeve cap to the jacket armhole stitching line. Hand-stitch with a doubled beeswaxed thread.

Position covered shoulder pads and stitch in place. Bring the neck facing over the pads and hand-stitch securely.

Partial Linings

As on pattern instruction sheets, partial linings include the sleeves and either the front facing covering the upper shoulder area or an extended facing that covers the entire front of the jacket. A back facing often covers the upper shoulders in either of these. The extended facing is often used on ready-to-wear jackets to give them "hanger appeal" and is an excellent choice for lightweight fabrics and jackets that have set-in sleeves.

A "true" partial lining, as found in men's tailored sport jackets, has lining in the sleeves, across the upper back, under the armholes, and into the upper front chest. The advantage of this partial lining is that sleeve linings are easy to attach completely on the machine. See page 38 for cutting directions.

Complete the jacket shoulder and side seams. Insert the sleeves, headers, and shoulder pads as for a fully lined jacket (pages 82-83 and 85-86). Join the back and front extended facings at the shoulder and underarm seams. Finish the inner curved edge.

Sew the sleeve lining underarm seams. Place ease threads around the cap, if necessary, and insert the sleeves into the facing armhole. Join the facing units to the jacket; press and turn.

To machine-stitch the lining and jacket sleeve edges together, reach up under the extended facing and into the sleeves, between the lining and jacket fabric.

Partially lined jackets need well-finished interior seams.

Grasp the two seam allowances with right sides together and pull the entire unit back through the underarm opening. Stitch as for bagging the lining as described in this section.

Working from the right side of the jacket, align the facing and jacket underarm seams and stitch in the ditch for 1/2 in., following the steps for bagging the lining, as described in this section. Hem the jacket.

Buttons and Buttonholes

Choose buttons according to size, color, and style to complement your jacket fabric and design. Buttons with attached shanks are decorative; buttons with visible eyes give a more tailored or informal look, but they still need to have a shank fashioned so the jacket will hang correctly when buttoned. Spending a lot of time perfecting bound or handworked buttonholes isn't necessary, because professional-looking buttonholes can be made on the sewing machine.

Attaching Buttons

Jacket buttons need a shank, either attached to the button or made with thread, to hold the button slightly away from the fabric. When the jacket is buttoned, this shank is what holds the upper fabric from the other side of the jacket. The button should allow the buttonhole to move rather than flattening it tight to the jacket. Follow the pattern guidelines for button size, so that overlap and underlap will align correctly.

1 *Creating space between the jacket and button allows for a thread shank.*

2 *You'll have a well-placed keyhole buttonhole after Space Tape has been removed.*

3 *With a buttonhole cutter or seam ripper, slash the opening for the buttonhole.*

Mark button placement after buttonholes are cut: Lay the jacket flat and align the two front edges, facing sides together. Push pins through the buttonhole opening, 1/8 in. from the end, into the button side of fabric. Use the seam gauge to check spacing from the front edge and to ensure that button markings fall on the center-front line.

Working from the right side with two strands of beeswaxed thread, anchor the thread with a few small stitches. Remove the pin; stab-stitch the needle back and forth from the jacket top to the facing side to attach the button, then wind the thread several times around the base of the shank.

For buttons with eyes, place the large end of the point turner between the button and the fabric as you sew on the button (**1**). Remove the point turner, hold the button away from the jacket, and wind the thread tightly around the stitching threads. Button eyes should align with the buttonhole.

End at the facing side. Secure the threads with several small stitches taken one over the other. When you hold the jacket front flat, the buttons should stand up, away from the fabric.

Horizontal buttonholes are most common and begin 1/8 in. past the center front, toward the front edge. Place vertical buttonholes on the center-front line, to repeat the vertical lines of a fabric band or a row of topstitching on the front edge.

Working Buttonholes

To find the buttonhole length, measure and add together the button diameter and thickness, keeping the minimum length at 1 in. for better scale with the jacket.

Experiment with buttonhole sizes, different threads, and using Fray Check adhesive before working buttonholes on your jacket. Use layers of fabric that duplicate your jacket.

To mark placement, pin the pattern on the right jacket front, matching stitching and finished hem lines to the jacket's finished edges. Pin-mark the buttonhole placement, then pull the pattern away, leaving the pins in the fabric. With a seam gauge, make sure the pins are evenly spaced.

Apply Space Tape marking tape, and remove the pins. The colored horizontal and vertical markings let you space each buttonhole evenly from the front edge. The stitching length only goes up to 1 in.; lengthen it if necessary by adding more tape to the end. Stitch the buttonhole through the tape; tear away the remaining tape (**2**).

Apply Fray Check adhesive to the buttonhole's inner edges before cutting: Pin horizontally across the end of each buttonhole, then slash from the center to the pin with a small seam ripper or buttonhole cutter (**3**). Work carefully and slowly to avoid cutting the buttonhole threads or fabric.

Weekend Jacket Techniques

Once you've made several jackets, you'll feel comfortable with the process method and the many options available to you. Your efficiency and speed will increase, and you'll be able to make a jacket in a weekend or less! Make yourself stay on schedule so you get your jacket finished—and have fun!

Pre-Weekend Organization

1. Buy fabric, pattern, and notions.
2. Study and revise guide sheet.
3. Preshrink fabrics and interfacing.
4. Pin-fit and alter pattern.
5. Cut and mark fabric, interfacing, and lining.
6. Fuse all interfacing.

Day 1

1. Pin and sew as much of the jacket as you can: darts, center-back seam, front and back facings, and pockets.
2. Press, including pressing up sleeve hems.
3. Finish pockets and sew in place.
4. Join front to back at shoulders and side seams.
5. Press.
6. Sew facing units to jacket.
7. Stay the chest/neck area.
8. Press, trim, and turn front-edge seam.
9. Press and hem jacket body.

Let garment hang for at least one week so you'll forget about any mistakes. Your jacket will look great when you come back to it with a fresh eye. Wear it with pride.

Day 2

1. Sew bias hair-canvas strip to ease sleeve cap.
2. Sew underarm sleeve seams.
3. Press seams and shape sleeve caps.
4. Hem sleeves and insert them in jacket.
5. Add sleeve headers, if necessary.
6. Place and attach shoulder pads.
7. Sew lining together, then bag lining.
8. Make machine-made buttonhole and sew button in place.

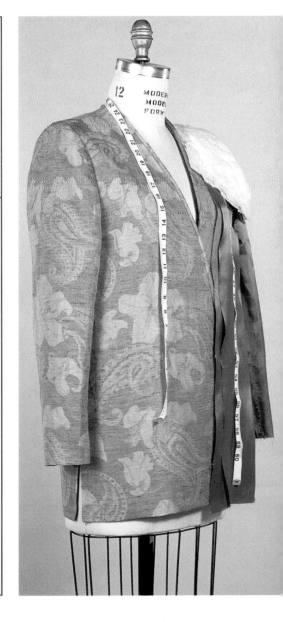

Index

M

Machine basting, 51
Machine stitches:
    discussed, 51-52
    edgestitching, 51
    machine basting, 51
    staystitching, 51
    stitch in the ditch, 51
    topstitching, 51
    understitching, 52
Mat, using rotary cutter with, 22
Measurements, discussed, 12-13
Microfiber, as jacket fabric, 17

N

Needles, for sewing machine, 22
Notions, discussed, 22-23
Nylon, as jacket fabric, 17

P

Patch pockets:
    attaching to jacket, 69
    curved, 68
    discussed, 39
    lined, 66-67
    lining pattern for, 39-40
    sewing of, 66-69
    template for, 22
    unlined, 68
Patterns:
    adding width to, 27
    adjusting, 26-28
    assembling tissue of, 26-29
    choosing, 6
    lengthening, 27
    multisize, 13
    pinning, 29-30
    refining, 24, 30-37
    shortening, 27
    See also Pin-fitting.
Pattern weights, discussed, 22
Pencils, marking, discussed, 22
Pens, for marking fabric, 22
Permanent basting, described, 50
Pin-fitting (tissue pattern):
    at abdomen, 28
    to bust, 27
    at center back, 28-29
    to chest, 26-27
    darts, 27-28
    discussed, 20, 22, 25-29
    at hip and side seams, 28

    to shoulder, 26
    at sleeve, 29
    to upper back and shoulders, 28
    at waist, 28
Pinking shears, discussed, 22
Pins, extra-long, discussed, 22
Piping, for jacket lining, 98
Pockets. *See* Patch pockets.
Point turner, discussed, 22
Polyester, as jacket fabric, 17
Pressing. *See* Construction.
Process method:
    discussed, 46-48
    for fully lined jackets, 46, 48
    for partially lined jackets, 48
    for unlined jackets, 48

R

Rayon, as jacket fabric, discussed, 17
Refinements to pattern, discussed, 24. *See also* Adjustments to patterns. Patterns.
Rotary cutter, defined, 22

S

Seam allowances, grading, 61
Seams:
    finished, 52
    flat-fell, 54
    Hong Kong finish, 54, 55
    mock flat-fell, 54
    mock welt, 53
    plain, unfinished, 52
    serged, 52
    welt, 53
    widening allowances of, 28
Shoulder pads:
    discussed, 21
    for kimono, raglan, and dropped-shoulder sleeves, 94
    for set-in sleeves, 39, 89
Silk, as jacket fabric, 17
Size, and pattern selection, 12-13
Sleeve caps:
    adjusting ease of, 40, 84
    folding pattern to reduce ease of, 41
    preparing, 82-83
    reducing ease of, 41

Sleeves:
    anatomy of, 40
    completing the lining of, 101
    dropped-shoulder, 10, 90, 93
    inserting headers into, 88
    kimono, 10-11, 90-92, 94
    preparing to sew, 78
    raglan, 10-11, 90-92, 94
    set-in, 10-11, 82-83, 85-86
    ready-to-wear vent for, 79-81
    styles of, 10
    vents for, 79-81
Space Tape, defined, 22
Square corners, sewing. *See* Corners.
Stab stitch, described, 50
Staystitching, described, 51
Stitches. *See* Hand stitches. Machine stitches. Specific types of stitches.
Stitch in the ditch, 51
Straight Tape, defined, 22

T

Tailor's dauber. *See* Dauber.
Thread, discussed, 22
Topstitching, described, 51
Transparent ruler, 22
Turn of the cloth, defined, 61

U

Understitching, described, 52

W

Wearing ease. *See* Ease.
Wool, as jacket fabric, 17
Woolens, defined, 17
Worsteds, defined, 17